BIPOLAR HEAD

Published by Dragonfish Publishing

© Peter Radnai 2024

Email: bipolarhead88@gmail.com

First published 2024

Paperback ISBN: 978-1-7635169-0-8 Australia

Cover: Photograph and hand-colouring by George Radnai, courtesy of the author.

Printed and bound by Amazon KDP, USA

BIPOLAR HEAD

A Snapshot of Life with Bipolar Disorder

PETER RADNAI

For my mother and dear daughter.
Both of whom I love more than words can say.

And in memory of my dad
who will always remain in my heart.

I would also like to dedicate this book to the memory of my cousin Joshua Levi
and Aaron Shaul, both of whom were taken too soon.
You are loved and greatly missed.

CONTENTS

ACKNOWLEDGEMENTS

Firstly I would like to thank my family and friends who stepped in and got me the help I needed when I took off on my first mania. I'd also like to thank the medical professionals who have looked after me since my bipolar one diagnosis. Thank you Professor Parker AO, Dr Wiren, and Dr Chin.

To my family, who I know suffered having to deal with me when I was elevated, I love you all, and can't thank you enough for your love and patience in having to deal with me at my worst. Ann & Ian, Les, Betty, Shmoo, Chana, Malka, Pnina, Ben, Mel, Peter and Henry, and of course Josh who we all miss dearly.

James Guiney for taking an excellent photo, Jimmy, you are the definition of a true friend. The first to step in when I needed to be told to just shut up and take my meds!

To my other friends who have been there for me, I can't thank you enough. Friendship is not to be taken for granted and I am blessed to have you in my life.

Cuz DJ Law, thank you for saving my arse on many occasions in and out of court, and for all of your advice.

To my editor Becky Gurevich, a huge thank you for taking on this project and mentoring me through the pages. I could not have done this without you.

Julia Reingold, I don't think I could have finished this book without you. Your skills, and belief in this project enabled me to get it done. Thank you for your work and friendship. I will always treasure your short stories, and friendship.

To my Dearest Dom, I love you with all my heart, I am so proud of the amazing woman you have become.

Dear Dad, thank you for taking the photo of me which I used for the cover, and thank you for all your amazing photos, which today are great memories. You were more than a photographer. You were a true artist. Thank you for showing me that it is more important to follow what you love to do for your living, than work as a slave for the dollar. You were the funniest man, making everyone laugh and smile all the time. I love you and miss you so much.

Dear Mum, You have been the toughest person I have ever known. You define the meaning of tough love. But you have always been there for me when I have been at my worst. You are the ultimate survivor, and my hero. I love you.

PREAMBLE

I'm bipolar.

I didn't choose this. It chose me. How lucky am I! Yeah, right, my fellow bipolar beings are thinking. This is a curse. Yes, sometimes it is. Other times it is a blessing.

I can't escape this; I can't deny this. I just have to accept it.

I have accepted this now. It's only been 26 years. Twenty-six years of acceptance. Learning and trying to see that this is not some kind of punishment from G-d, it is in me, and I can't escape or deny it.

Those that know me well can tell right away where my energy is at. As for the others in the community that know me by acquaintance, well, they wrote me off as crazy years ago when I totally lost my mind during my first manic episode.

A lot of people don't get it. There is a huge stigma with mental health. Sadly, people judge, and once tarnished with a mental condition that can really scare and frighten people, it's hard to get that label removed. I know that everyone in my community knows I have this condition.

Not to worry, it's not their problem or concern. I need to deal with it and make sure my life has mental balance. Throw me the juggling balls, long knife, and fire-stick. Some days that's exactly what it feels like. Other days are just perfect, things couldn't be better. Then there are the dark days and weeks that can roll into months of pain and self-torture. I can swing from the best highs to the darkest of depressions.

This condition is a mixed bag each day. It's certainly not boring, and it doesn't define who I am. That is why I would like to share these stories with you.

Looking back at past manias, I can say there was a lot of adventure and misadventure. Along the way, this caused damage to relationships, bank accounts, work opportunities, my own personal reputation, and time lost in places I didn't want to be.

There was also poor judgement due to the fact I was not thinking straight while manic. Mostly when I look back after a mania it is like seeing the damage from an emotional tornado that has flattened relationships instead of houses and some possible dreams. Then I see the damage to my finances caused by a lack of self-control, or a belief that there is going to be some kind of new source of funds, so it is okay to spend up big. But money comes and goes. Physical and mental health are priceless.

These days, when I feel an elevation coming on, I just lock myself in my home and ride it out. I can't stop it, but I can limit the damage by staying in my safe place and let the meds do their thing. Eventually, I can get on with life again outside my house.

These stories are about my life with bipolar disorder. For 31 years I was fine. Always a positive person. I loved being a drummer, gardener, surfer, those things were always a great release of energy for me. But after a monumental shift in my life and some emotional trauma, I cracked. The years that followed had me in and out of psych wards, due to seasonal manias and the horrific and sometimes suicidal depression. It was a long journey back to understanding this condition and adapting myself to accept and move forward.

Fortunately, depression is not in my brain now. I fear it may return or I may have to wrestle and fight that demon again someday, it is just par for the course with bipolar.

People look at us with bipolar disorder and don't get us. They mostly don't understand our mood swings which is fine. There is a stigma associated with the condition. But it is unfair to judge someone when you have no idea what they are experiencing.

Sometimes not even the doctors who treat us know how we feel, not in the core, but they do know how to prescribe the medications today to help manage the ups and the downs. The good ones also have advice on additional things you can do to help move you into a better headspace.

I'm sick of having to explain myself to people who don't understand the condition. Why I have so much energy in springtime, or why I'm up at 1.30 am after getting only three hours of sleep, with a head full of extra antipsychotic meds to shut my brain off. It's hard to understand and live with but, if I can't sleep and have had a good attempt at it, then I will gladly take the three hours of sleep that I had, knowing I will have to pay back my sleep debt to the lords of slumber at some stage, but for now I can't just lie on my bed tossing and turning full of energy.

If I happen to be in a downward spiral or mood and I don't want to talk to you, it's not because I don't love you. I just need to be on my own to get back to feeling better. It is the worst. I have come through this many times. When the negativity takes a hold of my brain and makes me shut down, I lose all desire to do anything.

Trailing along the floor of a depression is the worst. But I know until I turn it around, get myself moving, doing the things I need to do, I will wallow in the mire of mental hell.

Being able to say that today I am fine is huge. It is all that matters. I am grateful for that. But I am guilty of taking it for granted when I am well, because it is such a brutal path back from depression.

I have done it more times than I care to count.

I'm tired of taking medication but realise that without it, my life can become unbearable, not just for me but for my family and friends.

It's okay for you not to understand me. You don't have to get it, friends, and family. Doctors and all.

Having bipolar disorder is no joke. I have learnt to take it seriously. If I don't then I'm going to end up in a bad place.

Oh, and don't worry, I will catch up on my sleep debt. I wish I didn't have to, but I will. Bipolar is not a superpower, although there are times when I think it is.

There is more to it and a lot more for you to read so I am going to leave it here and say: Family, I love you. Friends, I love you as well. If you have bipolar disorder and are reading this, you are also my family. I want you to know BP can be a fight from the trenches, and an everyday battle. I'm not happy every day, but who is? And while it's not sunny every day, if I am struggling, I understand that things do get better.

This is my story. It took a long time to write. I started writing this as a diary for my therapy in 2002 but the time feels right to put more of my experiences on the page.

I also want to thank my family for putting up with me during my crazy moods up and down, and I especially want to make a special dedication here to my mother and dear daughter. Both of whom I love more than words can say. I also would like to thank my treating psychiatric doctors, as well as the ambulance drivers /paramedics and the police, for not tasering me or shooting me when manic when they have been called in to haul my arse away.

Mental health

It is the inner space that can take you to happiness or hell on earth.

INTRODUCTION
Feel The Fear and Do It Anyway

This is a hard one.

This is the hardest thing I have ever done, exposing myself to you. Getting these words down was no small feat. It's a hard story to tell but in my most recent elevation, I have to say, I got off lightly. It was a mild one that ended in a broken heart and some shattered dreams. This time there were no police, no psychiatric ward, just a change-of-season mania. I was running on gas tanks that just refused to allow me to recharge. But that's mania.

It runs its course but even with the extra medication to help me get to sleep, I was only on about three to four hours a night. Not good. Being sparked with the additional excitement of a wild romance didn't help, it just took me even higher.

It was early August 2021 and things were going well. There definitely was damage from the spring mania of 2019. I can't go into that here because it is way too personal and the emotional damage to loved ones was brutal.

This milder mania was fuelled by a wonderful woman, who in the end left me shipwrecked, just south of love island, on the reef of broken hearts.

If only there was a pill for heartache.

This mild spring mania left me feeling naked and exposed. I bore my heart, my life story to a brave woman who is a fighter in her own battle. Nonetheless I was left feeling that I had yet again, revealed my bipolar condition to someone who maybe I shouldn't have.

It had been a magnificent month filled with laughter and great conversation. We had a full-blown passionate and exciting love, the kind you see on the screen.

I do love the odds of a challenge, but this was going to be really hard from the get-go. For starters, we don't even live on the same continent. She may as well have lived on Venus, while I'm stuck here on, a bloody big island, a million miles away from her in Australia.

Love can make people do crazy things, and with my new-found energy I'm surprised I didn't beg Elon Musk to lend me his plane so I could go visit her. But the reality was, I was stuck. I had other commitments here in Sydney as well. As an only child, I'm now the full-time caretaker of my 97-year-old mum who is a holocaust survivor. I probably could have arranged for some respite care, but Covid made it impossible to leave. She was also stuck. Apparently, they had Covid on Venus as well and what made it worse was the fact that neither of us were vaxxed.

Then the reality set in. We both crashed. During this time, it was the Jewish high holidays. A very powerful time of reflection, prayer, and asking for forgiveness. I was praying for the world to make it through the pandemic, but we also realised that as good as it felt, our love was not to be. Not for now anyway.

She went back to try work it out one more time with her boyfriend, and well, I was still elevated but in control, meaning I was in my safe place where I could wait for the mania to wind down, with the right dose of meds helping me.

The mania was not her fault. That was waiting in the wings desperate to turn up the dial, but the thought of being with her and the prospect of a future with her took me to another level. I was off and running.

I was absolutely broken and bleeding out badly. Days had passed since I had heard from her. Eventually, she broke the silence and replied to my email. The one line that stuck with me was *'feel the fear and do it anyway'*. With these brave last words, the warrior Venetian goddess set off into the sunset, (possibly in a tow truck).

Being still a bit elevated, I spat and cursed. I was super pissed off, but I can't deny I still love her. So, I will take her words of encouragement, feel that fear, and finish this book.

If you have bipolar disorder, I have one message for you:

Be good to yourself.

Life, as we all know is hard enough. Most of us have issues with our health, mental or otherwise that is not of our choosing. Having bipolar disorder certainly adds another layer of complexity, sending you to euphoric elation, then down to the darkest lows.

The good news is the medication available today has played a huge part in managing the condition for me. How much medication, and what medication is always the question, which goes hand-in-hand with having a good psychiatrist. Having mental self-awareness, in other words, being aware of where my headspace is at, has been something important that I've had to learn.

I now know the feeling when mania is coming on, but I'm always surprised at how long it takes for my brain to spin back down to a non-elevated space.

As for depression, the only words to describe that are like being in hell on earth. Sadly, I know when that feeling is coming on as well. It's like sitting on a roller coaster making the first climb up to the top. I know where I am mentally, and I don't want to be strapped in for the ride down, but I know it's coming. There's only so much further up I can go before I plunge. I can see the descent and I am helpless, there's no getting off. Then just like that I am ripping down that ride at 100 mph into the pit of darkness, pain, and misery.

Once the depression takes over, I am paralysed in that horrific darkness with what seems to be no escape or way out. I have to ride it out, survive on a day-by-day basis, and pull myself out from the quicksand of despair. If you think that sounds a bit dramatic, let me say that it is not even close to how bad or desperate the body and mind can become. Although now I know what to expect and can slowly make my way out after a period of binge watching every show on Netflix. Yes, there is some mindless joy to it.

If I visualise the end of the darkness, I can then work towards it and finally it becomes bigger and brighter, and life can slowly continue again. I crawl out of that quicksand that is depression and begin to re-engage with people and my life. People say there's light at the end of the tunnel, but they don't tell you that often you have to go down and find it. Sometimes you even have to light it yourself.

Keeping my mind in a good space takes work. I can be my own worst enemy; sabotaging my life with stupid decisions when things are going great, deceiving myself or just being inactive in making sure I am on track in my life. All these things play a factor in the state of my mental health.

Then there has been the drug and alcohol addictions. As much as I loved the feelings they gave me, that is something that I have had to give up as it has been a huge detriment as well in my life.

I can't blame myself for having bipolar disorder. When the mania kicks in I know I am helpless, and it is something that is not my fault. How I deal with it from that point makes a huge difference in the way I recover from those elevations, and same on the other side, should I unfortunately sink into a depression.

Today I have many stories of manic episodes in my life, as well as depression, and recovery. I didn't choose bipolar, but I have had to accept and learn to live with it. In these bipolar chronicles, I am sharing some of these stories with you.

I also want to note that my bipolar has the classic traits of the condition. The energy up and down pushes everyone with this condition to crazy highs and crashing lows. There are some common traits of manic energy, and depression, but we behave and express this in our own way. Sometimes in control, other times totally out of control. I think that is the hardest thing for people to grasp. If it's not taken seriously, it will destroy you. I don't want to be too dramatic, as I mentioned this can be managed.

But always remember if you have this condition it's ours to own and make the most of. Use it to your advantage, even when you're at your lowest, never give up. The bad days pass, I promise you.
Remember, life is about staying in the game.

Catharsis

The process of releasing, and thereby providing relief from, strong or repressed emotions.

CHAPTER 1
Sleepless Again

31 December 2015
Summertime Sydney, Australia

It must be close to 3 am and while I've had a micronap or two, I just can't seem to get down to some serious REM sleep. I don't even know what I am thinking about. Actually, that's not true, I am simply thinking about one thing and that is, *here we go again... another summer mania.*

I'd like to get back to sleep but it's not so easy. Nothing is when you have bipolar disorder. Please don't get me wrong, at this stage of my life I know I must follow a game plan which includes my daily regime of medication. Tonight, I've taken more than my fair dose of medication, enough to sedate a small village and I am still wide awake. The good thing is, it's almost 2016, so staying up means a new year and hopefully a better year is only a few hours away.

Back in 1995, before I was diagnosed with bipolar disorder, the options were totally different. I had a source of endless energy that would fuel my days and nights. I wanted to go out and stay out. Manic energy can be a wonderful and useful tool to getting a lot done. But if it's left to run for days or even months on end, the result will only be grim. Back then, I never needed an excuse to head out. I just wanted to be anywhere but home. I would go out at night until all hours. That may have been undiagnosed mania, but I wasn't having the tell-tale signs that I now know when my moods swing to the manic side. Staying at home with hypomania running through my veins is never an easy task but back then, I think it was the flaming youth that drove my passions for the night.

I was born in the suburb of Bondi in Sydney, Australia. My parents were both immigrants who got married later in life, my father George being 40 and my mother Elisabeth was 38. Both being of Hungarian Jewish descent, they suffered terribly at the hands of the Nazis, as well as the brutal antisemitic Hungarians who rounded up the Jews into ghettos before shipping them off to death camps or used them as free labour in Hungary. I heard many stories during my life about the abuse my parents went through. I tried to imagine these horrors, but no matter how hard I tried, nothing could come close to living through such a horrific experience. Nonetheless, my parents moved as far away as they could, to Australia. It was a great new beginning for them and their friends. It lacked the culture of Paris where my parents spent five years after the war, but they loved their new beginning, and their new life on the island so far away from the horror of their youth.

I was too young to remember my first Bondi death experience, but it happened to be on our front doorstep. We lived in a house next door to a large block of flats in South Bondi. My father loved his morning paper and while going out to get it, found a dead man in our front yard. He had been stabbed and thrown over the fence onto our property. After that horrific incident, my mother wanted to get away from this part of the hood, so she had us packed up and we moved to my second house not far away in North Bondi.

I really loved living in that first house because we had great neighbours who lived across the road. They had a pool and I remember my family joining their friends most weekends for summer barbeques and partying while I spent hours in the pool. I loved being in that pool with my floaties on my arms and big egg-shaped Styrofoam™ bubble strapped around my waist. Those first two years were fun. I was loved and look back on those times knowing I was happy. At this point I had no brothers or sisters, so I was the focus of my parents, and learning how to share came much later in life. My parents worked hard. My father was a photographer and my mother worked in jewellery sales in a shop in the city. I spent a lot of time also being raised by my grandmother Seraphine. She was the only one in our family who kept kosher and observed Shabbat. Although, my parents always had Friday night dinner which was special, followed by an evening at my Uncle Ziggy's house. I had my beloved cousins, Ann and Les who are like my siblings, or the closest thing I have to siblings.

When I was six, we moved one more time about a kilometre away to Dover Heights. This was the family home and is still the home where my now 98-year-old mother lives. I moved back home to look after her in these most tender years. But make no mistake, she is still a tough fighter which is why she has survived so long. My mother and I always had a deep love, but we had many fights over the years as well. I felt it was the right thing to do by being here to look after her, but coming back to Sydney was not always a great place for me. I do love and appreciate the fact I was born in such a great part of the world. But it also was the place where I had some of my worst times.

In the '60s and '70s, Bondi was a real working-class surfside suburb with a mix of Aussies, New Zealander Maori, and my tribe, Jews. Not far away, about a 15-

minute drive, was the redlight district of Kings Cross. There were a lot of drug dealers and sex workers that worked in the Cross area at the time but they lived in Bondi. Back then, the place had a lot of charm and great appeal but if you were looking for trouble it was never far away. There were no young couples pushing baby prams around or expensive European cars parked all over the street like today. Bondi has always been a rough diamond. Don't be fooled by the pretty veneer of the ocean and seductive white sand; people die in Bondi every year. Someone usually goes into the surf, and someone might end up having some kind of mishap on the land. It is just the nature of the place which is alluded to by the Aboriginal meaning of *Bondi*, 'water tumbling over rocks'. In the '90s, there was a notorious gay nightlife which would sometimes, heartbreakingly come to a screeching halt as gangs would attack some of these men and send them plummeting down the rocks. Yet, millions come to visit this great beach not knowing of the dark side or mishaps that seem to go down every year at this tourist mecca.

Tragically, early one morning at 7.31 am on the 28 June 1997, a French freelance photographer named Roni Levi had a manic episode on the beach at Bondi and began wielding a knife in front of police. He was shot by the police, right there on the sand, in broad daylight and was fatally injured. Roni was only 33 and in a full-blown manic episode. He didn't have to die. He was waving around a large kitchen knife but that was no reason for the police to shoot him dead. It's devastating that the only way the police could deal with the situation was to shoot Roni. There was a rumour that those cops were out all night getting high, and that they made bad decisions, tragically ending in death for Roni. For me, it was an eerie reminder of the first time I had experienced a psychotic episode that strangely also came to a crescendo on the sand at the very same place.

CHAPTER 2
Mania Number One: Breakdown On Bondi Beach

December 1995

It could have been November for all I knew, I don't seem to recall the date, but it was the start of summer I know that for sure. I was working at home in my study while my girlfriend at the time was sleeping in the bedroom. Seemingly from nowhere, these questions started to fly into my head. Strangely, the answers came immediately. My surprise quickly turned to fear when I realised that I could hear the answers. How could I hear the answers?

I couldn't focus on the work I was doing because these questions were just flying into my head at a million miles an hour. As soon as a question came into my head, I heard the voice give me the answer right away. What was more interesting was the fact that the answers made sense to me. Thought after thought, I began to feel as if I was under some kind of mental attack. Just where this cerebral bombardment came from was a mystery to me. It didn't dawn on me for many hours, but I eventually realised that the voices that were answering my questions were indeed coming from my own mouth. I was stunned. The only thing I knew for sure was that this was not normal. Looking back with what I know about myself now, I can admit that I was having a psychotic episode. Voices in my head, audible voices... I think that is an apt description for the word psychosis, not that I knew the meaning of that word at the time.

Just like everyone, I have had good and bad days, but this night my life was about to change in a way that I would never forget. From this night on, I was going to learn a lot about who my friends really were and discover a painful truth that I really did not want to accept about myself. Sometimes the truth can really cut deep. And look, if you really wanted to, you could live in denial about a lot of things. But when it comes to your health, it is a reality that you must face head on. Especially when it is a matter of life and death. Bipolar can be a killer, taking the lives of about 10-percent of people who suffer from the condition. If you don't accept the reality of life with bipolar disorder, then you're playing a game of Russian roulette with your own life. Not to mention the chaos and turbulence of what bipolar can throw at you. If you fail to accept the condition, then it will suck you into a cruel whirlwind of ups and downs, over and over until you finally realise that something needs to change.

Of course, no one wants to admit that they're losing the plot. We all want to know we're in control of our mind, our decisions, and our actions. But when it feels like your head is in a pressure cooker, it becomes harder to take some positive action and face the reality of the situation. I know from my own experience that it just becomes too overwhelming to face the music and change the things that are in my control. But it's far more challenging if you're already in a manic or psychotic state of mind. What may seem to be a good thing for you during an episode isn't usually the best thing for you in reality. Mania starts to make your brain spin faster and faster. You don't even know it at first. You're feeling great. You might as well be snorting cocaine; it releases the same feelings of euphoria. But that night back when I was 31, I wasn't snorting coke, well not that night anyway. That night I sat at my desk trying to work away on a project that I was trying to finish. The attack of questions that flooded my mind was no ordinary distraction. We all like to think that we are in control. We like to think that we make smart decisions, and our thinking is correct. Being unwell in the head is what happens to other people. Or so I thought.

CHAPTER 3
A Little Chat On The Beach

Time had evaporated. I'd been at my desk getting nothing done and I wasn't tired at all. The audible voices now had my attention. I'd been sitting there for hours; I'm talking at least seven or eight. I'd lost track of the time, it was still dark outside, but it was now the early hours of the morning. Where did the time go?

I just couldn't stop these thoughts from flying into my head. I was freaked out of my mind; it was all too much to comprehend. Soon the questions turned into instructions. It seemed as if the voice didn't have to prove itself to me anymore. It had my attention, and I had no control over it. I was told to go to the beach; this day was not going to be my best day at the beach by a long shot.

I was living in Bellevue Hill, a wonderful, leafy suburb not far from Bondi Beach. With the sun about to come up, the voice in my head insisted that I go to Bondi Beach. This was not my idea; it was an order I couldn't ignore. I was *instructed* by the voice in my head to go down to the beach. This clear command kept coming at me over and over. It wouldn't leave me alone, I couldn't escape it, so I did what I was told to do. I wish the voice of common sense and reason would have told me to go to bed instead. I think my whole life would have been different, but I felt I had no choice. I thought immediately that what I was experiencing was some kind of supernatural experience. That perhaps this was G-d talking to me, or some evil inclination. I was beyond terrified; it's an experience I would not wish upon anyone.

That morning, the drive from Bellevue Hill down to Bondi took about five minutes. The day's sky was turning from dark to light, but the sun had not yet come up over the horizon. The sky was overcast and the air warm and humid. As it was getting lighter, I began to wonder if the sun was going to make an appearance at all. I arrived at the beach and parked the car feeling completely muddled. I had no idea what was going to happen. My mind was grappling, trying to understand what was happening to me. I did know that it was not normal and was also something completely beyond my control and comprehension. The voice was in charge, I was totally at its mercy. There was nothing I could do to stop it. When I tried to clear my mind, it came back with even more intensity. I was thinking maybe I could laugh it off or wind my mind down with a joint or some Valium. But you can't wind down a psychotic episode. There is no going back from the doorway of craziness. The whole situation was beyond my control, my reality was so blurred I didn't know what to think or believe.

I parked the car and walked down towards the water. There weren't many people there yet. I walked until I reached the wet sand and started pacing up and down the beach. The sun was coming up over the horizon, it started to appear in the clouds over the rocks at the northern end. It was as if the sun was putting on a private screening for me. There were small waves breaking onto the shore, and as I looked at the sun, I felt a connection to the universe. I felt as if the sun was confirming all the thoughts I'd had earlier. The voice commanded me to keep looking at the sun. This was easy to do at first as it was heavily overcast and filtered, not the blazing ball you can only glance at for a second. Soon, I tried to look away from the sun but the voice which I now wholeheartedly believed was coming from a godly source, was telling me to look back. I tried several times, but it was hard. I was frightened and began to cry. Now, the sun and the voice were both inescapable.

The questions kept on coming, now along with the answers. Things that were going on in my life. It was all too much. I kept walking on the sand, crying hysterically. I wasn't embarrassed, there weren't many people on the beach, but it must have looked weird, if not totally insane. This was the most overwhelming experience I've ever had, and one I will never forget.

I was out in the open with nowhere to hide or turn. I didn't want to have any part of this Q&A, but I was in deep now and there was no going back. The questions kept coming as I was walking on the wet sand. When I refused to believe the answers that came into my head, (and believe me I did not want to take these answers for being the truth), a wave would push up onto the shore to my feet with what seemed to be an additional surge, a bit like an exclamation mark just to rub the point in. It was as if nature was working in harmony with the answers and the waves were reiterating the truth. The sun was not going to be out for much longer. The heavy clouds were beginning to close in on the sun and all the voices in my head. I can safely say it was one of the most frightening experiences I have ever had in my life.

The intense Q&A had a lot to do with things that were going on in my life, and things that were going on in the media at the time. I had just submitted a lease for a new place to live and the voice told me that I was going to get the place, which I did end up getting a week or so later. I was also told that my mother was going to win the lottery. About a week later, my mother did win twelve thousand dollars on the poker machines. Not exactly right on the money, but for me that was close enough. It was just another confirmation from what I had been told that morning on the beach. I was also told that the upcoming federal election at the time was going to be won by the Labor party and our new prime minister was going to be Paul Keating who was the leader of the party. This also came true from the prophetic session that day on the beach. No surprise to me that he did. I was getting some other messages as well, but my brain was like scrambled eggs.

In the weeks that followed I felt that I had some kind of special communication. I felt that I was indeed a prophet and was now totally convinced that I was some kind of Messiah or a madman. I chose to think that I was indeed the Messiah. Looking back now, I am pleased to say that I am indeed no Messiah or prophet but at that time during my first full-on psychotic mania, I had totally lost it. I didn't want to be anything other than a regular person with the usual desires to do well. But if I had a choice to be anything or anyone with some kind of special gift, then naturally I would want to be someone who could use my new information to make the world a better place. There were no other specifics on how I was going to achieve any of this. For now, it was about faith. The voice just wanted me to believe that I was the vessel chosen, and naturally I believed there was more information to come.

Things did seem to calm down on the beach. I managed to compose myself enough to get in the car and make it back to my place, but I was absolutely shaken. I felt like I had been stirred more than the oxygen tank on Apollo 13. Remember the one that exploded? That was me. Now I had arrived back home and had to explain all of this to my girlfriend at the time. It was not easy. I remember her trying to calm me down but there was not much hope there. I was beyond rattled.

As a Jewish man who grew up with very little Jewish education, I really knew nothing about my religion except for the fact that we have a few holy days a year, a lot of laws and commandments as prescribed from the Torah on how to live our lives, and some religious Jews dress in a funny way. I do believe that the world was made for a higher purpose, man was not put on the planet to just destroy it. Inside I always believed no matter what, good will overpower evil in the end and that is that. But it was hard for me to believe this growing up. Hearing stories from my parents and grandmother who lived through the holocaust, and death camps. How could I really believe that the world was a good place knowing that my parents went through this unimaginable hell on earth. If the Jews, as some people say are the chosen people, I would only ask myself, what are we chosen for? To be hated, discriminated against, and rounded up like animals to be exterminated? How could this world be a good place? It was impossible to believe, because even in the Torah the stories, trials, and tribulations of what the Jewish people had to go through seemed just too much of a test of faith. I think that is why my parents may have not sent me to a Jewish school for my education, or why my parents didn't keep kosher or keep the Sabbath after surviving the holocaust.

During my first psychotic mania, I did not want to believe that I was going to have some special powers or be The Messiah for the Jews. I was out of my mind, frightened. I didn't want the task to save the Jewish people or the world. I had clearly gone over the edge, forced to believe the voices in my head and it's difficult to give any proper explanation except that to me it was very real, and it seemed like I had no choice.

Back at my flat I was talking at a million miles an hour to my girlfriend. She had no idea what to do, she called my friend who I call Sticky Fingers, and told him to come and see me. I was going to see him, but it was about 9 am, and after almost a two-hour break, the voice was back at me. I was ordered to go get on my push bike and start riding. I knew Sticky Fingers was on his way, but I had to obey what the voice was telling me. These were now instructions I did not want to follow through on but felt I had to.

I had no choice in the matter. I was hesitant to get on my bike, but the voice became so frightening, terrifying, I had no choice. I did as I was told and got on my bike. The worst part of this was, I had no idea where the voice wanted me to go at this stage. What was I to do? I resisted the voice to the point where I couldn't take it anymore. I was panicked, and then my worst fear did come true. The voice commanded me to start to ride towards the cliffs of Dover Heights.

Dover Heights is where I grew up and the cliffs above the ocean are about 2 kilometres up the road from Bondi Beach, just up the road from my parents' place. I had always walked my dogs there as a kid and if you follow the coastline, about 3 kilometres away was the notorious spot called The Gap. The Gap was a cliff walk about 90 metres above the ocean at the south head of Sydney Harbour. It's a notorious suicide spot where people would breach the fence and take their lives. I can't say anyone has ever survived that, but thankfully today it does have video surveillance and better fencing to make it harder for people to climb over the fence.

I got on the bike, and I started to ride towards the cliff, fearing the worst. Was this now becoming a test of my faith? Was this my Abraham moment? Was my faith in the Lord to be tested? Why of all places was I asked to go to the cliff? Surely, on arriving there the next command was going to be one that I might not be able to come back from. When Abraham was asked by G-d to walk into the furnace, he came out alive and unharmed. His brother thinking that he could do the same was not as fortunate. Nonetheless, Abraham walked into the furnace and survived. I am not Abraham, but I had no doubt that the voice I was hearing was G-d talking to me, so I had to do as I was asked. I began to cry as I could not believe I was being ordered to do this, and of course I was terrified. For the record, I have always believed in G-d and while not being religious or having the education, I didn't want to find out at the end of a 90-metre leap of faith. I was certain I had no feathers or ability to fly so things were not looking good.

Still bawling my eyes out as I rode on towards the cliff, the thoughts of what was to come next only made me feel even more hysterical. Am I really going to be asked to jump off the cliff? I mean what would I do if the voice commands me to jump off? Would I really disobey the word of G-d? I would have had no choice but to do just that. Quite simply, I was shitting myself.

Riding towards the cliff, tears streaming down my face, was one of the most frightening things that I have experienced. But then something amazing happened. The voice gave me a new instruction. It told me to ride to my other mother's house. My second mother, Mama Ruth, was the mother of one of my closest friends Dr Paul. I met Paul at the age of six and we bonded as closely as kids could. Don't ask me why, but at the age of six I asked Ruth to be my mother. I mean this with no disrespect to my mother, but Mama Ruth has always been a special person in my life. A great mentor, a woman of strength, who spoke six languages, had an amazing life story of her own, but was also a person who showered me with love. She was a person who I could always rely on for an unbiased opinion. I was relieved that I was no longer told to go to the cliffs.

When I got to Mama Ruth's I ran inside, babbling in a delirious state of mind. She must have thought I was totally mad, a crazed person, someone who was in no way of sound mind which no doubt I was. We had a chat over a cup of tea, and she did calm me down somewhat, and then I left. After a short ride on my bike, I was home. Sticky Fingers had been and gone and I arranged to meet up at a café in Kings Cross. I first met up with Mr Sticky's partner. Sticky was coming in a little while, but when Mrs Sticky Fingers saw me and heard me babble and rave on about my experience, she literally ran away in fear. I terrified her with my newfound experiences and who can blame her? I can't remember exactly what I told her, but I told her I had a crazy prophecy and maybe even that I was the Messiah. All I can remember is her eyes lit up in fear as she realised that things were not right, and she ran off down the road from the madman. She must have contacted Sticky Fingers because he rang me on my cell phone and told me to meet back at my place. He arrived and I told him about the amazing things that were about to happen. I was in the full flight of mania. At this point I must say I felt kind of relieved. He didn't seem to be as frightened, more amused I would say.

Sticky Fingers and I played music together many times. Naturally, with a name like that he was a keyboard player. We both had a love for the same bands, and we jammed a lot at my father's photographic studio with a host of different musicians. We also did business together and had a love for all things pot. For now, I felt as if I had passed the test given to me by G-d. The scary voice had not demanded anything from me, so I was beginning to relax a bit with this whole experience. I was confused, but still doubting things in my mind. I can't really say what I believed for sure.

Sticky Fingers then told me he was going to put me in a hotel for the night. I think he wanted to put me somewhere, so I was going to be safe. Well spare no expense for the Messiah. He booked me into a suite at the Park Hyatt Sydney with a room facing the beautiful harbour with an amazing view of the Sydney Opera House. As I walked into the hotel, I remember tipping the staff 100-dollar bills. Handing out about four of them. Money was not going to be a problem for me anymore because I was the Messiah, so why not be generous and pass some around!

Later that night, one of our close mates Brian joined us for dinner. I was being loud and over the top, Sticky Fingers found it hilarious. As for Brian, he was so freaked he ran out in the middle of dinner convinced I was nuts, leaving me with my girlfriend and Sticky to finish the meal. Sticky said that people were looking over. They might have heard a thing or two that may have sounded weird, or just downright crazy. We continued to eat our dinner and we all laughed, having a great time. We were lucky not to have been ejected from the hotel.

That night, I stayed up all night. No need for cocaine. I was so charged I could have lit up a street. I did have my bong and I was smoking a lot of weed, self-medicating all night. This was my second night and I still had not slept. Feeling manic can be such a great feeling, it's easy not to sleep. In fact, when elevated I hate the thought of sleep. On this night, there was no way I was going to sleep either. The manic voices in my head were having a great conversation and I was tuned in for the show.

CHAPTER 4
I Love A Great Hotel Room

Since I couldn't sleep and I had this amazing view, I was going over what happened, trying to work out if it was real or my mind playing games on me. I really did believe it was real. I felt agitated and just smoked more weed to soothe it, but I was not doing myself any favours. There was no way I was going to get to sleep. The voices kept coming as well. I was looking out onto the harbour from this great suite that Sticky Fingers put me in. I didn't care that it was night two with no sleep. It didn't even dawn on me, nor did I feel tired.

It was coming up to about 6 am and the boats on Sydney harbour looked fantastic. It was the start of a great day. I saw a JetCat that was taking people from one side of the harbour to the city. The JetCat is a fast, slick catamaran. Then I looked at some tugboats that were out in the harbour as well. The voice in my head said, 'You like the JetCat, it's fast and sleek looking, then it said, 'look at the tugboat. It's slow but never forget that the tugboat is much stronger. Be like the tugboat!' Seriously where did that come from? I liked the analogy; it made good sense to me at the time.

It was now around 9 am, I was in a deep mania, and I rang my father. I was never short of words or conversation, but this time my dad knew something was wrong with what I was saying. I was venting about one of my cousins, going on about it like a madman. The way I was talking was different and he knew it. My father, not knowing what to do, asked Sticky Fingers to get me to the hospital. Not just any part of the hospital, the psych ward at Prince of Wales Hospital called The Kiloh Centre.

My father George (in loving memory, R.I.P.), said he was going to meet us there which he managed to do. But there was one thing that we had to do on the way to the hospital. I had to stop at my bank to give Sticky some money that I owed him. I did mention that Sticky and I loved our weed, but Sticky also knew how to grow the first hydroponic weed that I had seen. I became a client, a wholesale customer. I did two years at horticulture school, I really had a genuine love and wanted to learn all things horticulture, but I especially wanted to know how to grow killer weed. It was the beginning of the indoor pot growers, and my friend knew exactly what he was doing. I could move as much as he could give me, and everybody wanted his fantastic northern lights indoor strain.

Sticky and I arrived at the bank and then something very strange happened. I went up to the counter and asked to make the withdrawal of the cash from my account and the lady at the teller told me that every computer in the whole of the banks' network *in the whole of Australia* was down. As I had been working in Information Technology for about seven years, I found this hard to believe. No, I found it impossible, and naturally I just thought it had something to do with me. Somehow, my secret powers influenced the banks' computers, and this stopped me from making the withdrawal. We decided to wait. After about 30 minutes, we finally got the money, and we got moving to our next destination: the Hospital.

CHAPTER 5
Welcome To The Rubber Room

We entered the psych ward, and I don't think that I realised that I had been taken to the psych ward. I thought I was in some kind of general admission, emergency, or something. We sat and waited. I wanted to leave but my dad and Sticky insisted I stay. There is only one way you can end up in a psych ward in Sydney. The first is if you commit yourself. The second is if you're deemed unwell, posing a risk for the community or yourself and you've been taken in by the police or ambulance.

I sat waiting. It seemed like ages, but finally a doctor came out and said he was ready to see me. I had no idea that I was already in a locked ward. The door to freedom was already 80-percent shut. During the initial interview with the psych doctors, I wanted to make it out of there fast. I was only there to make my father happy; I had things to do.

The doctor asked me some probing questions. Do you know why you're here? How have you been feeling? Why do you think your family are concerned? I remember trying to cut to the chase, so I thought I would tell the doctor that I had some prophecy I wanted to share with him. I told him a few things, one being who was going to win the next federal election. Probably not the wisest move. I should have just kept my mouth shut. I was not going to reveal what I had experienced down at the beach and my little bike ride to the cliff, as I didn't know this doctor person, so why should I share the truth about my new insight and alter ego? They called in another doctor now. The stakes had been raised. They spoke to me, but I just wanted to get out of there. Besides, I refused to believe these expert doctors and junior brain care specialists. I was arrogant, because I felt totally charged with what I believed to be my higher power, and I had no doubt about it. But I had enough insight to think that if I told them about my little conversations I was going to be in some kind of tricky situation.

I sat there and all I wanted to do was get out and get on with my life, especially now that I had been handed such wonderful insights and tasks from our creator. I still couldn't turn the thoughts off. My mind was racing, and I knew what was coming my way. Some of these thoughts were clear, some uplifting, others were frightening. They were often confusing, but it all seemed so real. I had no doubt about that. I just couldn't work out why I had been the one chosen to be the vessel for all of this, but I had no control of the thoughts. They just kept pouring into my head.

It was now day two of my enlightenment and it was impossible to stop the ride. I felt as if I had so much to do, but I was stuck. What was taking these doctors so long? Why can't I get out of here? I might as well have been waiting to be processed to go into jail. Sitting there, I could not stop thinking about how frightening the whole experience was, yet at the same time it was like I had been chosen for some mission which was yet to be revealed. Yes, there was some prophecy, but was that even going to happen? It was like a teaser for the bigger things that were going to be uncovered. But the truth of the matter was my freedom was about to be taken away from me. This was my first trip to the laughing academy. I was sitting in a locked ward, not that I knew it at the time. I just wanted to be released so I could get out and continue with my life.

Little did I know that the doctors had other plans for me.

CHAPTER 6
Time To Take Your Shot

Waiting around was beginning to really push my patience. The agitation of two sleepless nights was settling in and I was still in a state of disbelief that my path was now chosen, not by me but G-d. A role I will say I didn't want to accept but felt I had no choice. I just didn't want to be terrified by those frightening voices that were going to command me to do things I didn't want to do, let alone make me prove my loyalty again to the supreme power of the universe.

Sticky Fingers was sitting outside the examination room with my father. They must have been in a state as well after having to deal with everything. While I was thinking that my life was about to go on an incredible upward trajectory, they were sitting in the waiting room, wondering if I was ever going to return to earth.

The doctors finally came to the conclusion that I needed to be contained in the cooler for a forced vacation. At this point there was no turning back. There was no way I was going to be let back out into society that day. I was walked down the corridor and they asked me to walk into a bland room with no furniture. One window had some very unattractive grills on it and in the corner was a thin gym mattress about the size of a single bed. One might think that the classic rubber room would be padded from floor to ceiling to ensure that the guest du jour would not harm themself in case there may be some kind of disagreement with any advice the doctors may care to prescribe. No, this room was a rather cold space, no padding on the walls either.

I had been asked to enter here and looking around, I was beginning to think this was not going to end well. The Judo mat on the floor really didn't look comfortable either. While I propped myself on the thin mat, waiting for something to happen, in walked the medical cavalry. Now in the room, there were three doctors and four burly orderlies. They told me I was not going to leave, and I was being booked in for what some might pleasantly call an 'unexpected vacation.' I saw that these guys meant business and it seemed to me that I didn't have too many options. The burly orderlies grabbed me and held me down on the mat while the doctors told me to calm down and accept their poison dart. They told me in no uncertain terms that I was going to receive this loving injection whether I liked it or not, so there was no use in fighting it.

Well, I went off. I started to curse and try to get up, but I was overpowered. Even with my superhuman manic strength, these burly guys held me down, so the only thing I could do was warn them and boy did I give it to them. It was like a scene out of *The Exorcist* without the head spinning 360 degrees and minus the vomit. I do recall saying to them that if I do not wake from this injection then there was going to be some nasty horrible curse on all of them and their families and this rhetoric was intense. It was not me. I was going crazy thinking that they were going to kill me with whatever it was that was loaded up in the injection. My yelling and fighting continued, my cursing becoming even more intense. After about five minutes of this yelling and resisting like a man possessed, Sticky Fingers popped his head into the room and shouted, 'Pete just take the needle and shut the f- up!'

Sticky was always the voice of reason, a man I could trust. I finally stopped resisting and they injected me with the brain lock known as Accuphase and I was out like a light.

CHAPTER 7
Welcome To The Locked Ward

When I came to, which was some time the next day, I woke to find myself in a private room. I had no idea where I was, but I was no longer in the non-padded rubber room, and I woke in a haze in a single bed. I was so out of it. I was mentally paralysed and had no energy or control of my body. I don't think I even had the energy to scratch myself. I looked around and could not believe that my guardian angel Minko was there. He said, 'Come on Peter, get up we are going, I am here to take you home.'

I was so out of it, I heard what he said but I couldn't move. That darn drug was so powerful, I could hear but I just could not get up even if I wanted to.

Minko, an Israeli and former IDF soldier, really was my guardian angel. How he found out that I was in this locked ward I have no idea and still to this day I have never asked. But he was there, and he repeated himself, 'Come on Peter. Get up. We are going!'

I remember him repeatedly telling me to get up, almost yelling, but all I could do was look at him. Drooling was about all I could do. I then heard a doctor who was also in the room. I don't think I even noticed he was there until he started talking. He made an alternative suggestion. He said, 'You don't have to leave, I can give you a blanket if you like and you can stay here.'

I looked at the door, which was only 2 metres away, and was contemplating my walk to freedom, but there was no way I could get up or even move. The option of the blanket sounded so much better and as much as I wanted to leave, I said to the doctor I will take the blanket and that was it. The doctor knew the pharmacological brain clamp had done its job. I was temporarily paralysed. Unknowingly, I had sealed my fate and was now going to have my first fully paid vacation in the laughing academy. Had I known this at the time I would have made more of an effort to get up, but that drug I was injected with completely shut me down. I could hardly open my eyes. The only way I was going to get out of that room and hospital was if I was carried out on a stretcher. Yes, I was now officially a new client in this special unit for the mentally unhinged. I took the blanket and passed out.

When I woke up from my drug-induced coma, the reality of where I was, began to sink in. This was way more serious than I could have imagined, not only was it a small ward, I found out that this was actually a locked ward. There were doors behind other doors, and a corridor that had dorms and some single rooms. The was a TV room, a nurses' station, and a small courtyard. The ward had about 20 of us inmates and I was pacing around this small space thinking, *How on earth did I get here*? It wasn't jail but it sure felt like it. How was this part of G-d's plan for me and the incredible insights I had down at the beach? All I could think of was I had to get out to make those plans happen. I also had my business which needed my attention. But now, I had bigger problems than that. I had to learn how to play by this new set of rules. Their rules. Because my life as I knew it, my freedom and everything that existed outside of these tightly locked and guarded walls, was my new reality.

The big question of course was not so much, how do you cope in there with your newfound friends and new environment, it was even worse. How on earth do you get out of this nut house? In life we all have our plans and goals. Everyone has different dreams, tales, and experiences, but there is nothing worse than thinking that you're doing okay, and then waking up one day in a situation against your will. I was always an outgoing person and a risk-taker. A person who believed that you must follow your dreams and go for it. But now my life as a free man was taken away from me.

The hard-core drug I had been injected with had worn off now, but I was still (in the eyes of my keepers) a manic person who needed to be sorted out; taken down a notch or four from the elevation with various medications that they said I had no choice but to take. There were no options in here. In this new home away from home, the rules are not yours and it is not an option to disobey. If you do, it's back to room 101 with the mat on the floor and the nasty needle known as the 'do not argue shot'. I had to conform.

Worst of all, I found myself to be in a scary place from which leaving seemed impossible. How long were they going to keep me? The people wandering around these wards seemed in worse condition than myself. I found my new friends to be fellow bipolars, manic or severely depressed; unipolar depressed and the ones that seemed to be in more mental anguish than the others in that ward; those that were suffering from schizophrenia.

The high walls in the courtyard and two locked doors meant the only way out was a green light from the doctors who would have to believe that I was well enough to be let back out into the free world. They had deemed me as a danger to myself and society. I found out after a day of questioning, that the only way out of there by early release was to present my case in front of the magistrate. Yes, they hold court inside these locked wards and by no means is this a *kangaroo court*. It is a legitimate courtroom, and a magistrate comes in to preside over each case with the doctors on one side and yourself on the other. You can be assured that the doctors present their side of the story quite convincingly, which is not going to present you in a good light.

They just want to keep you locked in for at least another two to four weeks until they know they have worked out their exact diagnosis and a medical regime. One that not only brings you back into a normal mental rotation, but also ensures you're not going to end up back in the laughing academy after being freed.

I don't blame the doctors. They have seen mania many times and believe me they had no doubt in my case, I was as manic as they come. Looking back, I must agree. I was totally manic, with auditory hallucinations. In my state of full-blown mania, being out in the free world was only going to lead to more tears for me or someone else. They were just doing their job in preparing their case to the judge as to why I should not be let out. As soon as I heard about court and the opportunity to be freed from this mental prison, I only had one question: Could I have my lawyer come down to represent me? The head nurse told me that of course I could have my lawyer defend me. 'It's a proper court. You have the right to defend yourself, or you can have representation.'

Well say no more, I saw a glimmer of hope and finally a way to get myself out of this place. I asked the head nurse again, 'This is a real court, right? Like outside, yeah?'

He said, 'Yes, of course it is. The doctors can't keep you if the magistrate thinks you're of sound mind and not a danger to society.'

I immediately contacted my lawyer from the only link to the outside world – a coin-operated payphone. I told him that I didn't care what plans he had in two days, he was coming to the hospital.

'I am having a hearing and you, my dear lawyer, are representing me and getting me the f-out of here.'

My lawyer agreed and said he would be there, for a nominal fee of twelve hundred dollars. I had two long days to kill in the ward until my day before the judge. It took a lot of getting used to my new environment. I am a positive person and I do make friends easily, but in an acute psych ward it's not easy to start up conversations. Firstly, my mind was dealing with the disbelief that I had ended up there in the first place. Secondly, I didn't believe that I had anything wrong with me, so I was in full denial. Besides, I wasn't there to make friends. Thirdly, I still believed I had this higher purpose, not a clear mission, I was thinking that the Lord was going to reveal that to me in time. In the back of my mind, I was still believing the manic thoughts.

I was full of manic energy pacing around the small ward and biding my time with mindless TV, or whatever I could do to distract myself until my court date. I couldn't concentrate enough to read. It was a very harsh reality. The truth is the doctors do not want to keep you there any longer than they need to, but they knew my head was not right and they needed time to work out a regime of medication that was going to not only bring my brain back into a healthy state, but also what my body was going to be able to tolerate. They were taking my blood daily and giving me Tegretol as a mood stabiliser and a heavy antipsychotic called Zyprexa that was my slow down med, while they figured out the best regime for me.

CHAPTER 8
Here Comes The Judge

Finally, the day came for my court hearing. I met with my lawyer, and I told him I had just spent the last of my money placing ads for a new computer component and buying stock to sell. I think I sunk my last 40K into this. I had placed all my money and hopes on this being a winner and a new product that was going to be successful for my business.

Court day arrived and my lawyer and I went before the judge and the doctors presented their case. My lawyer presented my side of the story, and I was awarded my freedom. I was ecstatic to be getting out of there, but it wasn't certain just yet. Prior to me being released, I had to meet one of the two heads of psychiatry. This is standard procedure for all patients prior to be given the green light to leave. I will never forget what he said to me.

He said, 'Peter, you don't realise this, but you're not well.'

I looked at him and I said, 'You will never understand what is going on, but I am sorry to say that you're wrong.'

Then he just said, 'I have to release you but I'm afraid to say you will be back.'

I smirked and, in my mind, just brushed off his comments, thinking he was arrogant and had no clue. I mean, he was only one of the head professors of the most prominent psych wards in Sydney, if not the country, what would he know? I walked out of his office and then the hospital. I was a free man.

CHAPTER 9
The Smell Of Freedom Was Great Until...

After receiving my final tick of release by the professor, I was out. I could now get on with my life after those crazy few days in the laughing academy. I can't tell you how good it felt to be back in society, able to get on with things in the free world.

Just like in my prophetic visions, I got the lease and keys to the new house my girlfriend and I wanted to rent, and we moved in. I was given scripts of various medications, I can't recall what they started me on, but it was an antipsychotic and some mood stabilisers for sure because I enjoyed the calming effect of the meds at night. The medications did help with the racing thoughts as well, but I was in total denial of the new title that they had given me which was a diagnosis of bipolar type one. I refused to believe that I had anything wrong with my brain. It is one of the hardest things for anyone to accept. I wasn't trying to ignore the professor's words as I left the prison of the mentally unwell, I just could not accept this new label. Who wants to be labelled with any kind of illness, especially mental illness?

Now I had to make my plans work. I had my new product to sell, the ads were in and so was the stock. With my new lease on life, I started to plan what to do next. I went with my girlfriend up to the Blue Mountains to look at properties to buy. My plan was to sell the stock that I had and then with that money put down a deposit on a new home. We found an incredible sandstone house on a large block that was part of a former dairy farm. There was a huge shed at the back which had fantastic wooden sleepers on the floor. It was perfect as my music room, office, gym, and there was also plenty of room for my girlfriend to have her art studio as well. The house had so much charm and in my mind, I was already moving in. However, in life sometimes things just don't work out as planned. As the saying goes, *Man plans, and G-d laughs*.

The Blue Mountains was going to be a great environment for myself and my girlfriend. Quite a bit cooler than Sydney, but just over an hour's drive from the city so I could be close enough to my family. After all, I had a 5-year-old daughter, and I didn't want to be far away from her or my parents.

During my late teens, my only ambition was to be a professional drummer. While I was playing gigs in bands around Sydney and working a day job, I did manage to do two years of a horticulture course as I mentioned before. Once I found a band that offered me a full-time gig touring around the country, I packed in horticulture school and off I went to play music professionally. At this point in my life, my days of being in a band were behind me. I just wanted to make it in business. I also had a passion, I loved growing plants, especially growing pot. As mentioned earlier, my dear friend Sticky Fingers was one of the early adaptors of growing indoor hydroponic weed. We're not talking big commercial grows, just a regular sized bedroom that had been filled with flood and drain tables, and lights, growing using a method called *sea of green*. This method means you grow lots of plants from cuttings and putting them into a flower cycle early so you get these short plants that go into head very quickly. The only problem is you need to grow a lot of plants using this method.

I had the honour of being able to look after his crop from time to time and now he had gone away, and I was keeping an eye on things for him. I was a free man, but I was still elevated, and while I did have horticulture knowledge, I had never dried or cured pot properly before. Usually, he would give me the produce already dried in ounces ready-to-go. Growing weed is one thing, but if you don't dry it and properly cure it, you end up with crap weed that looks okay but doesn't smoke well. Sticky came back and the weed was ready to be pulled. He asked, 'Do you want to take the now ready crop, or do you want me to dry it?' I thought for a moment and decided to take it and dry it myself. We agreed on the price, and I took the freshly pulled weed back to my new abode. Being keen to get rid of it, I tried to dry it quickly. Well, that ended in tears. I had a sauna in the new house I was living in. I hung the weed in there, and it dried way too fast. I messed up. The pot looked fine, but it was not cured properly. Not only did I mess this process up, to make matters worse, it was now April, so all the outdoor weed from up north flooded the market and I couldn't sell my weed.

Now, I was thirty thousand dollars in debt and had no idea how I was going to pay for this costly mistake. To top it off, the computer product I had invested into with all my savings flopped at the same time. It was a perfect storm of failures. To say I was devastated was putting it mildly. I had a heap of stock of both products and no cash flow. I could not even give it away, let alone sell it. That not only wiped me out financially, but it put me into a huge panic. I was in a state, and I really began to freak out. My energy rapidly moved from being up and optimistic to a feeling of total despair and suicidal depression, the dark side of bipolar.

I had bills to pay. I owed thirty thousand dollars to Sticky and the rent and utilities bills kept coming in. Of course, we needed to eat as well. My thoughts became so dark, and I could not see a way out of my financial mess. The depression kept getting worse and worse. It was like I was being loaded up with weights and I could not move, think, or see my way out of this situation. I was experiencing bipolar depression for the first time. I had no idea about this. In the past I have had bad days as we all do, but this was worse. It was an awful feeling that I could not shake off and I had no clue what to do. Not knowing that depression usually follows a mania, I had no answers. Still in denial, I refused to believe my diagnosis. The voice I heard when I was manic, that was supposed to be my guiding light was nowhere to be heard. I really needed to hear something from my guiding light but there was silence from him. No words of advice, no positive reinforcement, nothing.

There were no solutions or even a bone thrown at me to save me from this terrible situation. I was stuck with pounds of garbage weed I couldn't sell, and a ton of specialised computer components that nobody wanted. I was screwed. My freedom now turned into big walls in my mind trapping me with nowhere to run. I couldn't escape the fear, I could hardly sleep; I was slowly getting more and more depressed. The bills kept piling up and each day I was heading well into a mental decline. I could see no way out and then I hit such a low that I did the most unfathomable, desperate thing I have ever done.

CHAPTER 10
Stop The World I Want To Get Off

It was a Friday night and I had to go to Shabbat dinner at my parents' place. I picked up my five-year-old daughter with my girlfriend and we headed over there. I had sunk into the darkest of deep depressions and this had been going on for a few weeks now. I just could not see my way out from this feeling or from my financial problems. I'd gone from being a successful guy with my own business to broke with debt hanging over my head. I have had some bad days in my life, but I could not recall a time in the past where I felt so low. It was the deepest depression I have ever experienced.

My mental health after my release from the hospital went from fine to not so fine, and as my plans and ideas melted away to nothingness, I hit my rock bottom. There was no help or guidance from the voice that was supposed to be my shining light. No more prophecy. It was just a world of mental pain and anguish. I felt completely broken. I was still in denial about my diagnosis and tragically, the only way I could see myself getting out of this situation was to take my life.

Friday night dinners at my parents were mostly pleasant. My mother was a very good cook and loved having us over. It was also a lovely way for me to enjoy time with my daughter as I had recently divorced. This Friday night however, I could not enjoy the dinner, my family, or anything. I was at my lowest. I had three bottles of pills at home that I was sure would do the trick, so I had made up my mind. I was going to take my life.

At the end of the dinner, I drove my daughter back to her mother's place, kissed her on the head and gave her a big hug as this was, in my mind, the last time I would see her again. I then drove back to my place, grabbed the three bottles of pills, downed them, and went to bed thinking that was it, my life as I knew it was about to end. In the morning, my girlfriend suspected that something was wrong. I had not woken up nor could she raise me from my sleep. She called my father who immediately told her to ring an ambulance.

My next waking moment was something I wasn't expecting. Instead of meeting my maker, I woke to a few nurses surrounding me as I looked up from a gurney. I was in a hospital and the nurses were pouring charcoal down my throat, telling me to keep drinking. I looked around, realising my desperate and stupid plan had failed and now I was being forced to drink this disgusting, thick liquid. I had no idea how long this had been going on for, but they must have been making me do this for a while. The shame of the situation set in. I was so embarrassed, but also completely out-of-it.

The liquid charcoal makes your tongue swell up, commonly called a thick-tongue. I tried to talk and answer the nurses who were asking me questions, but it was almost impossible. It seemed they could understand my replies, nodding their heads. They must have been fluent in charcoal-infused English.

I lay there looking up at the bright lights and the nurses and I remember feeling like such a loser. *F*ck!* I had no idea which hospital I was in or what was going to happen once they had filled up my stomach. Since I came into the hospital several hours after taking the pills, pumping my stomach was not an option. The force-feeding seemed to go on for ages. I had no idea of the time, but they must have been happy that they managed to save a life. I know I am grateful today that these charcoal force-feeding super nurses did bring me back. I wonder where they are today, if I knew I would love to say thank you to them in person.

I remember thinking to myself, '*What have I gone and done?*' as I lay there on the gurney. It was the lowest point in my life. Only a mentally unwell person would go through with the act of attempting to take their life. It's a terrible frame of mind to be in. To be so desperate as to see only one way out of a bad situation. Now, I had the added shame of this low act, but I felt helpless with no other alternative. Before deciding on drawing the final curtain, the only two things I felt were complete despair and helplessness. I can't be hard on myself for what I did. It was not a cry for attention. I had genuinely had enough of my life.

If I had been successful, (G-d forbid) who knows where I would have landed? Well, I suppose that's the million-dollar question. I don't think there is pizza and a chocolate fountain on the other side. What if it was worse? What if the other side was a few emotional rungs further down from where I was, and there really was no hope of redemption, or escape from that situation. I had to find a way of turning this around and I didn't have the answers. I did realise that being hard on myself was not going to help me. Working on the small steps to a happier place was the only way to start feeling good. Oh, and I know it's easy to say that from the perspective of a healthy mind, but to put it another way: Please don't do anything stupid like I did. It just might be an irreversible act. If you're in a depressed state, I can totally understand what you're feeling because I was there right before I decided to take those pills. When we are at our lowest, nothing anyone says can make us feel better. You can hear the positive words from friends, family, and your doctors and yet inside you just feel the pain. It seems like a situation that will never change. Although, if you stay in the game, the worm turns. Your life will get better. When you're at the bottom, feeling the worst emotions a person can feel, the only way is up. It must get better, and it will. Just hang in there. I know from my own experience that I have turned things around, not just once but several times.

I have healed from my depressed state of mind so many times. Then there is a period of calm when I am better, feeling great, and before I know it, I am going through another mania, followed by another crippling depression. My mood has changed from level, to manic and then depressed so many times I've lost count. After all it is bipolar, what goes up, comes crashing down. At other times, I might have skipped the mania and gone straight to depression, and as I slid down that slope, there was nothing I could do, and I could not believe I had sunk back into that horrific funk again. This is a hard pattern to come to grips with but that is how it goes.

Prior to downing those pills, I was done. I wanted out, and I'd had enough. I was over everything. The only way you can imagine how low that feels is if you have been at this point yourself. My heart goes out to you if you have or if you are there now. Like I have said before, I am glad I was saved in time and the nurses with their charcoal milkshake did their thing to keep me in this material world of pain and pleasure, and sometimes mediocrity, which is just fine.

Looking back, I am grateful that I didn't do my research properly because had I taken other things along with the three bottles of downers, I would not have survived. I do not recall how long I was on that gurney. It seemed like ages. The shame-metre was running at a solid 9.5/10. It is bad enough doing the act but failing brought on a whole other level of shame. I can't imagine how my parents, or my girlfriend must have felt. Naturally, they were happy I survived, grateful that I didn't perform the ultimate disappearing act.

Well, surviving was one thing, but it didn't help my mood. I felt lower than before if that was humanly possible. Of course, I realised I was in an emergency room, but I did not realise that after my life savers had done their fine work at keeping me here, I was in for an extended stay in the cooler. Yes, I was back in the laughing academy for another round of mental rehab. Only this time, it wasn't for the treatment of mania. It was for the worse side of bipolar disorder. The treatment of the depression. The horrific flipside of the mania, the worst side of this coin. As I lay there, I didn't realise I was already booked in for an extended stay. A four-week fully paid vacation in the field of dreams, *more like the field of despair*.

I lay there, dazed, with no idea of what was to follow. If I could have died from embarrassment, shame, and guilt, they would have left me there on that gurney and read me my last rights. Well, I am Jewish so the prayers for Moishe Ben Zev would have done just fine. In Judaism, when someone is sick, we pray for the person to keep them in this world. Maybe that's what was happening because I did not die of shame, guilt, or embarrassment. At the time I wished I had though. Yeah, I was unwell. It was going to be a long, slow recovery back from the dark side, a horrendous place.

I was taken back into a room well behind the locked doors to recover. I'm not sure if they gave me some additional medication but I passed out. When I woke up I realised where I was, the same feeling of despair came over me. The thought of my failed suicide attempt gave me even more to think about. Knowing that all my dreams and hopes of a comeback were now well and truly gone, and the fact that I was now back in the acute psych ward was hard to take on board. I didn't have that many choices left. Again, I questioned my thinking over and over. The voice that had terrified me, yet promised so much, was no longer guiding, or coming forward with any suggestions. I felt totally abandoned.

I was grateful that the year was not 1902 or earlier because back then it would have been a visit to the asylum with a huge *NO EXIT* sign on the back of that locked door. It dawned on me that back then the mentally unwell had very little chance of freedom and were locked away from society for good. Now in the modern era of treating mental health, I know that the doctors want to treat us with close medical care and supervision to help bring us back to a stable mind, and then when we are better, we are released. Today the doctors can work out the right combination of medications and therapy to help everyone that enters these wards to leave. They really don't want to keep people in there. Beds are always in high demand. It's not a fastfood restaurant and the patients are not in there for a quick meal either.

CHAPTER 11
Welcome Back

I wasn't planning this visit, but my actions and the fact I was thankfully saved by the medical staff, meant I was in for another stay. Very quickly I concluded that this time I wasn't having my lawyer get me out. Firstly, I didn't have the money, and secondly, I was so broken mentally I just had to accept my situation and what the doctors were telling me.

When it comes down to mental health we can only live in denial for so long. What can I say, the truth really hurts sometimes. It felt like I was never going to be happy again. My business idea failed, and I had blown the last of my money on stock and advertising the product in major PC magazines. The pot I had to sell was rubbish – I gave it to a friend to see if they could do anything with it – and I had a debt of about forty thousand dollars to Sticky Fingers. The shame of the failed suicide attempt and being back in the locked ward again took my mood even lower if that was somehow possible. It was horrific to be back in the psych ward with all my plans now well and truly shattered.

As I woke each day in the hospital, recovering from my failed exit from the planet, the daily routine felt like a grind. There was nothing that the doctors or nursing staff could say to make me feel better. It was a gruelling process to accept my reality and surroundings. To say that things were not improving was an understatement, it was punishing to accept where I was and how low my life had sunk.

All I ever wanted in life, after playing music professionally, was to work for myself. I had my lucky break, and I had a good run at both for a while. Maybe I failed the sustained pressure. Maybe I was a bad husband. The pressure of my marriage and my business partner who was also driving me crazy, led me down the path of self-destruction. It was the perfect storm that released the bipolar that was lying dormant in my mind, and I finally cracked. Now my business was gone. My marriage was gone as well. I have no idea why I was so desperate to gamble all my last money on that computer component. I risked it all, spun the wheel and it was a spectacular failure, and now I had lost it all. Along with my bankroll went all my hopes, dreams, and self-esteem. Back in '95, forty thousand dollars was a decent amount of money. It had to be manic behaviour taking a huge gamble like that.

Being so broken with no future prospects was destroying my mind. I never thought I could make it back to any kind of happiness in my life. The future looked grim, and that was me trying to be positive. For the moment, I just had to do as I was told. I listened to the doctors and took my meds. I obliged when they wanted to tediously draw blood from me every day. I felt like a lab rat and resented every waking minute of my situation. To make matters worse, I was sure that my recent activities and my current location had been spread around to people I knew in the community. I was convinced the word had got out and I had been labelled by all that knew me as someone who has lost the plot.

The stigma of mental health is horrible. Being labelled a crazy person, a madman, a nutter, or a person with a mental illness is very unpleasant to say the least. Once you have this label, you are certainly going to know who your friends are. The stigma of mental illness is real and extremely painful. Personally, I think eczema would be worse, but let's not compare medical conditions. Life might be like a box of chocolates for Forrest Gump, but here in the nut farm, my box of chocolates had turned into a box of turds. When it comes to health issues, everyone has something. We're not created to be perfect or to last forever. Our families leave us with a small genetic present. It's not a lucky dip. This bipolar gift was in my family and was just lying dormant waiting for its moment to shine.

People also love to gossip and in some sick way, kind of enjoy the fact that you have taken a turn for the worse. But people were not surprised. I lived fast and hard and loved it. Not all people were mean and those today are my real friends, but some were. Maybe they were just scared. People are frightened when it comes to mental health due to there being so much mystery and a lack of understanding of it. Also, the fact that there is no cure doesn't help, it's as if they think they are going to catch it from you. Those that are touched by bipolar get a very bad rap because manic people can be scary. I can be scary. Being labelled as someone who has lost the plot may be in some way appropriate, but it is not right. If we are manic, we are just not well. It is not our fault, please understand that. Today there is a lot of talk about mental health especially in the workplace but sometimes it is just talk with no real understanding or care.

Being locked up in the laughing academy, I could feel the words of the people on the outside talking about me in a negative way. I could just hear them saying, 'I knew it!'

'He was going to fall!'

'I knew this would happen!'

'He was taking too many drugs!'

'He was pushing the envelope!'

I knew those words were flying around out there and those words felt like daggers. I didn't hear them, but I could feel them. Were people taking joy in my fall from grace? I'm not going to say that for sure, but perhaps some were. In some weird way I could feel the negative talk affect me. In Judaism we have a concept called *loshon hora*, which on a spiritual level means that the two people talking badly about the third person are all affected in a negative way.

Speaking of labels, I was still coming to terms with the label that the doctors had given me as well – bipolar disorder type 1. This type of bipolar disorder they said was the most extreme version. They of course had a right to give my condition an official title. I didn't want it, but I had no choice. They are of course professionals, and it is hard to argue or dispute their diagnosis. I had proven to have prolonged manic behaviour, with the previous admission also having auditory hallucinations, then this was followed by a depressive stage, and a suicide attempt. Yes, they had enough symptoms to confirm my condition and new title. Me on the other hand, I didn't want to know or accept any of it. I really had no choice though. I was locked in the psych ward and was not allowed to leave. Not that the outside world had that much to offer. I had run out of ideas, cash, and plans. As for the voice, well that vanished along with everything else.

This time however, I was in no condition to refute my new title, nor was I in any way in a position to denounce it. I was broken. With nowhere to go on the outside except a world of shame and failed ideas. I was now a fully-fledged member of this esteemed group of the mentally unwell, and from what I had been told by the doctors, there was no cure, but the condition was manageable with medication. That was the good news. They told me that they needed to work out what medications were going to be best for me but assured me that they would get this sorted out before I was to be released.

This new title was something that if anything made me feel even worse. How was I going to be able to cope with this and carry this with me for the rest of my life? At the time I thought it was something to be ashamed of. Looking back, I was certainly ashamed of some of my behaviour, and yes, I probably had some apologies to hand out, that's for sure. But the new label? I certainly didn't sign up for it, nor did I want it. Apparently, it was my birthright, I already had bipolar in me. It just took the right amount of pressure and environment to make the condition reveal itself and when it did the result was a spectacular mess. I wish all that pressure could have transformed into some kind of diamond instead, but that is not how it works. I was in that acute ward thinking about my new title and of course running over what had happened in the events leading up to my attempt at ending it all. But really, that label? A crazy person? A madman? Nothing could have been worse than that title, well maybe an illness with a death sentence. Who cares if it is genetic or not. I didn't want to have to deal with this bipolar for the rest of my life. Surely, they must have made a mistake.

As a guy who has always had big dreams, lots of energy and a healthy positive attitude, being told you have a mental condition that can cause huge damage to your life if not treated with respect was something I could not come to terms with. I now had to have medication to keep me normal, I mean what is normal? That must be one of the worst things anyone can tell you. Being surrounded with my new friends, reinforced the fact that I had to take this seriously. It was hard to take anything seriously as I was so darn depressed. I kept thinking back on the events leading up to my great decline, and while I hate to be wrong like most people, I thought about that professor who signed my release. He was right. I was unwell. I thought I was fine, but I was unwell. Just as he predicted, I was back in the hospital. The professor had not seen me yet, but these young doctors surely had gotten their diagnosis right. Bipolar One. It was a brutal thing to have to accept.

Back again in my new home away from home, with my fellow bipolars, schizophrenics, and the severely depressed, the days passed very slowly. The food was mushy, waterlogged, steamed veg, typical hospital food. And finding some good conversation amongst my fellow inmates was hard to find. As each day ticked over, I tried very hard to accept my new title. It was a bitter pill to swallow, but I had to get used to it. I had to learn to accept the truth, and as we all know, sometimes we can't handle the truth. I had nothing else to do and nowhere else to go. So, working on understanding my new condition was all I had.

This time in the laughing academy, I had to behave and follow doctors' orders or else I might end up in the room with the mat on the floor and a sharp 'don't argue' needle in my arm. I certainly had no desire to go through that horrific experience again, and besides, I had no fight or argument left in me. I did think to myself, *maybe they got the diagnosis wrong. How did they know for sure?* In the meantime, the only thing I could do was to hope that they could work out which meds were going to help bring my old self back. I was desperate to get back into a healthy and happy space again and leave the academy of broken brains.

I have no idea what it is that drives a doctor to specialise in psychiatry, but I know one thing for sure that it's not the money. Without these warriors of wellness, the mentally unwell are never going to get better or learn how to manage their condition.

If this condition is not managed, the laughing academy becomes a home away from home, especially if one doesn't take their medication. I was told failing to be responsible with my meds would lead me back to this place. The locked doors would become revolving doors, and it is well known that bipolars and schizophrenics from time to time refuse to take their meds and they end up back in the psych ward.

Waking up in there every day was like groundhog day, the environment made me feel like a prisoner. My only escape was if I fell asleep and had a dream. This psych ward is separated into two locked wards. The smaller of the two wards is called the acute ward and the other is called the general ward. In the acute ward, there are two separate wings: women in one wing and men in the other. This locked acute ward is like a prison and escape is virtually impossible. I have never heard a story of anyone breaking out from there. The acute ward is where you are first placed so that they can keep a very close eye on you. It's a jail, there's no way of getting out, and noncompliance is not an option. It's where they take the wind out of the manic sails and the doctors and nurses begin your descent back to earth. It's now your temporary home, and it's not a pleasant environment, to put it mildly.

The general ward is a mixed ward with about thirty-five people. There are some other common rooms such as the dining room, and general recreational room with a TV, as well as a smaller TV room with a DVD player. Outside, there is a grassy courtyard with a pergola. Smoking is not permitted in the hospital, but people hide behind the pergola and light up.

The bipolars and schizophrenics, are usually wound-up, pacing around endlessly and sadly the severely depressed wander around with a hollow look in their eyes. I can't see why they prohibit people from smoking outside, it would make things slightly more relaxed. But most people try. If caught, the nurses confiscate their cigarettes. To them, this is all that they have. It's their only release or way to relax.

Back inside, the main common areas are also used for visitors and some creative activities. As I have mentioned, the psych ward is not a jail nor a prison, but there sure are some similarities. The courtyard for the acute ward has very high walls, higher than the walls in the general ward. It's impossible to break out from there. If you somehow manage to escape, or sneak out from the general ward, congratulations, now you are officially a fugitive. The police are notified, and it's only a matter of a few days before they catch you and bring you right back. Once safely back at the nut farm, you've lost your freedom and privileges again. You may have managed to escape for a brief period but now your time starts again. It's just not worth it.

Regarding the accommodation, in both the acute ward and the general ward, everyone gets their own room. But there is no ensuite, so we all share the various bathrooms available. During the day, I would spend a lot of my time watching movies in the small TV room. There were a few movies already there, but I was very grateful to have someone bring in some DVDs for me. I didn't have the patience to read. Watching those movies was a great time killer and distraction.

At night there was a 9 pm curfew. Prior to that, at about 8.30 pm, they served hot Milo which was a nice treat. This was followed by the nurses handing out the evening medications. I would stay up for another hour or so walking up and down the corridors, and maybe watching a little TV before heading to my room.

After two weeks in the acute ward, I was transferred to the general ward. The one good thing about being in the general ward, apart from being closer to my release, was that you were allowed to go out for an hour around midday. This was my first taste of freedom in two weeks. It was great to be able to leave and to be outside and watch the activity of the local shopping centre. I was also allowed to buy my own food, or personal items. I had to be very mindful of the time because if I came back late, they would not grant me my free time for a few days. When I came back from my short taste of the outside world, the reality of my surroundings quickly sunk in. I was still in a very depressed state of mind, and I was struggling to accept my diagnosis. Being amongst the mentally unwell was also hard to tolerate.

About ten days into my stay in the general ward, my treating doctor started giving me some positive and encouraging words. There was no specific date as to when I was going to be released, but the doctor did say it would not be more than another ten days. I was doing what they asked of me and behaved, keeping myself out of trouble, so this all worked in my favour. In my depressed state of mind, I tried to rationalise my situation and I even had some thoughts that this may be the best place for me for now. Not that I had a choice. I had to admit, it was a safe place to begin the slow path of recovery, even though it was not a relaxing environment.

My brain was still having trouble coping with my newfound diagnosis. I could not help but think about the past few months that lead me to two stays at the laughing academy. Those events will never be forgotten, and looking back was not going to make things any easier. Looking back can be fine in small doses, so long as it does not become obsessive. I know that it can be a part of the healing process, but overthinking the past is just going to make things worse.

The mania and psychosis were overwhelming and frightening, but my attempt at taking my life and waking up in intensive care, that was a whole other mess I tried to work through. I found it hard to clear my mind and find a way forward. The depression was still there and there was no counselling in the ward. Would it have helped? Probably. I know the staff wanted to treat the chemical imbalance first by getting my brain chemistry firing correctly. Those days went by at a snail's pace, and I could not see myself ever being a happy person again.

Visiting hours were daily between 4 and 6 pm. When my mum came in to visit me, which was almost every day, she would bring some sweets and home cooked schnitzel. I was always happy to see her. The food did help to lift my mood a bit, but there was a whole lot of soul searching that needed to be done. The drugs they were treating me with opened the 'secret hidden seven chambers of the stomach' and they had a huge weight gaining effect on me. Sure, the sweets were not doing me any favours, but the sugar rush felt good. Very quickly I worked out that comfort eating was not going to make my depression go away. The sugar hit was a poor substitute for a drug high. It did make things better for a moment but then the reality set in again when I jumped on the scales. I had put on 10 kilograms in just over two weeks.

CHAPTER 12
Depression Part One

If I thought about my situation for too long, where I was and the reality of my life in the outside world, it only made me sink lower. This was an inescapable headspace. I just couldn't fathom how someone could get back to being happy once they hit their absolute rock bottom. I could not see my way out. I was living in pure misery and felt absolutely broken. I had lost my Sydney privileges and the good life that I had, with no more second or third chances left to give me any hope or positivity. The stupidity of the suicide attempt had me back in the laughing academy at the full mercy of the doctors. I had felt that I was always a fighter, but for now I had no fight left in me.

It's one thing to attempt suicide, but to fail and wake up knowing your exit plan failed can and did make me feel like a loser. Well, a loser on one hand. On the other I felt like I had been blessed. Blessed that G-d, or some stroke of luck if you want to call it that, had given me a second chance to make a new life for myself. As I write this, I know I was blessed that I survived. It wasn't luck either. It was my destiny to have a second chance. The one thing I learnt was that no matter how bad things got, no matter how low I would feel in future depressions, I would never make another attempt on my life. No matter what life throws at me, I promised myself to stick it out. Even if it means just sitting at home watching endless hours of TV.

As I was told on that informal visit to the psych ward, bipolar depression is horrific. It is said to be worse than regular depression. In any form, depression is horrific, learning to have the patience to put up with it and not put any more pressure on myself is the most important part of the recovery. It's not easy to pull myself out from a depression. Getting through each day is hard. It can be a grind, monotonous, and boring. But there is nothing wrong with that. In this life it's not about winning, it really isn't. It's just about staying in the game. I think maybe on leaving the psych ward they should hand you a medal, break out the big brass band and throw a huge party. *You're free to go! We have restored you back to a level playing field. Hopefully we won't see you again!*

When leaving, there is no life plan, just a script full of meds and an appointment booked with my psychiatric doctor. I had to learn how to function again because I left that hospital in a fog of depression. Sadly, today too many people don't get a second chance at life. Too many people suffer not just with bipolar depression but regular bouts of depression. The western world has such high incidents of people with depression that it is one of the most common health problems around today. Raising yourself up from the ground is a huge upward battle, but I know it's possible. I have done it over and over and you can do it as well. Like I said, it is just a matter of staying in the game.

Going from manic to depressed is a vicious cycle, but the dark clouds will lift, and it does pass. It is hard to see at the time when you're going through it, every day feels like a battle because it is. I know very well from my own experience that even the smallest of things such as taking a shower can seem like an impossible task. Depression is the loneliest place on earth, and you feel that nobody understands or can help you to overcome this personal battle. My heart goes out to people who sadly didn't reach out to their friends or loved ones for help. I know I didn't prior to my attempted suicide. There is such shame and guilt associated with it, and some people don't have a close friend that they can talk with, or they don't really want to share how they're feeling. They just do the research, and sadly go through with the one thing that is irreversible. It breaks my heart. If only more could find the patience to ride it out and wait until the darkness lifts.

Because it does in time.

CHAPTER 13
Rewind... The Nervous Breakdown V1.0

The year was 1981, I was 17 and starting my last year of high school. My parents sent me to one of the best private schools in Sydney, Sydney Grammar School. It was a selective all-boys school that was probably one of the most expensive schools in Sydney. The school was steeped in tradition and was a very strict house of education. It's one of the oldest private boy's schools in Sydney and is near the centre of the city next to the Australian Museum.

For my primary school education, I had gone to a local public school called Rose Bay Public School. It was a co-ed school and I loved it there, the environment was relaxed and it's where I made lifelong friends. I suppose my parents didn't want to send me to the private Jewish school, Moriah College for some reason, but they wanted to give me the best education they could afford.

I was in Year 6 and had to write an entrance examination to see if I could qualify for Sydney Grammar. I remember going to the school and sitting the entrance exam in a very large and intimidating hall they called Big School. I didn't know what to expect when the letter finally arrived from the school, but I was accepted, and my parents must have made such a financial sacrifice to put me into that school. My family was middle-class and worked very hard. As mentioned earlier, my father was a professional photographer and my mother also worked fulltime selling jewellery in a shop in the city.

I had a few friends prior to being accepted who went to Sydney Grammar's Edgecliff Preparatory School, but they were in the year above me. I also knew a couple of other guys who were more acquaintances than friends who happened to be in my year. I knew these guys from a tennis camp which I used to attend during school holidays.

On the first day of Year 7, 180 boys assembled into the Big School Hall for our induction and orientation. It was one intimidating and overwhelming event I will never forget. We all sat on wooden pews, and at the front on the podium we were first addressed by the headmaster Mr MacKerras, whose reputation preceded him. He was a fine man and ran the school well. Behind him on the wall were large boards filled with the names of young men who excelled at the school and were academic recipients such as Rhodes Scholars, along with other students who were captains and head prefects of the school. After the headmaster finished, the head of Year 7 and 8 stepped up to the podium and introduced himself. He told us that he was going to read out our names and which class we were going to be in. I sat there nervously waiting as he started with Adams in class A, working his way down to class B, then C. By the time he worked his way through the D class, I was really sweating it. I had no idea how many classes were yet to be called, but this first day torture had to end at some point, I was a wreck. Welcome to Sydney Grammar School.

After the joy of the assembly, I caught up with the few guys that I knew who had transitioned from Sydney Grammar's Edgecliff Preparatory School. They asked me, 'So Radnai, what class are you in, A or B?' I looked at them and said 'F'. Well, at least they thought I was smart. Sadly, I was in the lowest class. Did I mention that the school had a very high standard of education? If I went to a public school, I would have been higher up for sure. But amongst these guys, the brightest of the bright, I was in F. On the positive side, I could only go up from here. It was a blow for sure. I certainly had my work cut out for me if I was to move up a class or two and that is exactly what happened.

I did work my arse off in that first term and after first term exam results were handed out, I was moved up a class to E. That E class years later produced a movie writer & director who did a little film called *The Adventures of Priscilla, Queen of the Desert*. Being a self-confessed non-academic, I am proud to say I did reach 30th in my year once for a biology exam, that was no fluke. The rest of the time I was always around 110th in the year; it was a hard school for me. I am not going to lie that the high academic standards of Sydney Grammar were a struggle for me. I did have some dyslexia and concentration issues, but there were other things there that I loved such as being the drummer for the school band, the sports, and the friends I had.

When we had our main mid-year exams, they handed out the results in the same torturous way in front of the whole year. We were all assembled in Big School, sitting nervously as they started to call out the names one by one. The torture of sitting there waiting for your name to be called with your result and where you were placed in the year was one of the most nerveracking experiences of my years at that school. The pressure really came from my fellow students. There were kids who had tiger parents, kids who were naturally quite intelligent, and the rest of the kids just worked their arses off.

In my last year of high school as the summer of '80-'81 began to wind down, I found myself getting worked up with anxiety and a nervousness like I had never experienced before. My father paid the first term fees, and I came back to start my final year of high school. I believe I was about two weeks into Year 12, and I just couldn't take it anymore, I was having a meltdown, so I ran away from home to one of my closest friends, Eben. My friend Eben's father was a tough east-end Jew who was like a second dad to me. He reassured me that everything was going to be alright.

'Just call your parents and tell them you're safe, but you're only going to come back home once they accept the fact that you want to leave school and get a job.'

I rang my parents, told them exactly that, and they agreed. I said I would be back in the morning. They must have been super pissed off, but I was in no mental state to go to school. I was totally freaked out, it was my first official meltdown, and just like that, my school days were officially over. That did bring me some relief. I know my parents didn't take the decision lightly, nor did they take me to a psychologist or psychiatrist for a mental evaluation. Had they done so, maybe my mental state would have revealed some traits that suggested I might have had bipolar. But I didn't show signs of mania, just a permanent worry and state of anxiety. On coming back home, I know I had to fulfil my promise to my parents and get a job. The job was going to be a means to an end as the only thing I really wanted to do was begin my career as a professional drummer.

CHAPTER 14
Following The Dream

In the Jewish world of careers and occupations, the list starts in position one with Doctor of Medicine followed by Lawyer, Banker, Chartered Accountant, and the list of careers rolls downward from there. Being a drummer is so far down on the list, I don't even think it gets a mention in the world of Jewish careers. While there are quite a few very successful Jewish drummers, including the greatest of all time, Buddy Rich, my mother was not thrilled about my career choice and was always on my case to start any profession other than drumming. I think my mother would have preferred any career over being a musician. After telling her of my aspirations all she said was, 'Drummer? *Drummer?* That's not a career!'

I will never forget those words.

My father never put a camera in my hands as he didn't want me to take over his business. I think if he saw that now everyone is a photographer with their phone glued to their hands he would say, 'Son, this is why I didn't want you to follow in my footsteps.' In a weird way he could see it all coming.

'Get a real job,' my mum would say.

And I would say, 'Mum this is a real job, I am being paid well and getting lots of work in the bands I play in.'

Then she would snap back, saying that drumming is not a career. She is one tough Holocaust surviving super mother with no filter, telling me exactly how she felt about everything. That was never easy, but I ignored her wishes to live a conventional, boring life with a day job that served nothing more than making a living.

I loved being on tour, going from town to town around Australia for three months at a time. It was a lot of fun. When I came back to Sydney, there were always the weddings and bar mitzvah's to play at; I was never short of cash. I also did some gardening work in between. 'This is my dream job,' I would tell my mum, not that she cared. To her it was not a career for her Jewish son. But I decided that I would give myself until about 24 or 25 years of age, and if I didn't have any success by then, I would go and get a regular gig, whatever that might be.

As promised, I got a job with my Uncle George (R.I.P.) who was a builder. He employed me as a brickie's labourer. My day gig was schlepping bricks from 7 am until 3 pm Monday to Friday, and at night I would be auditioning for bands that played original music. I finally found a band that took me in called *The Dreaming*. We played mostly original music, and a few covers. I got to do my first recording with this band as well, that process was so exciting to me, like most young bands, we did it on a budget and in world record time. The two songs we recorded were wellrehearsed, and being in a recording studio for the first time was an amazing experience. I was taking it all in. The engineer miked my drum kit, and the rest of the band's instruments and we were ready to roll. During that first session, we spent more time on the setting up and getting the sound right than we did on the actual takes of the songs. It was a great experience. We would play gigs from Thursdays through Sundays. I enjoyed playing with those guys, but it didn't last for too long. I think it was about six months. There was consistent work from a Jewish wedding and bar mitzvah band I played in. I was still looking for the next original band to join, but I met a lot of great musicians through this band. As the saying goes, *'a gig is a gig'*.

The Jewish wedding and bar mitzvah band was a regular source of work and they always paid well, not to mention, we got fed. Sometimes my father and I would know we were working the same function, but there were a few times when I went to play at a wedding and there was my father, who also turned up to take the photos. The apple doesn't fall far from the tree. Despite my father never wanting me to be a photographer, I loved playing music so the artistic side of me is there.

One Saturday night, I was out at the Hakoah Club which was the big Jewish social club in Bondi. In the big room where they held functions, I walked in and saw two guys with a massive keyboard and PA set up playing *New Order's Blue Monday*. My jaw dropped, they sounded fantastic, everyone loved that song, and they played it outstandingly. It was hard not to be impressed. I must admit I love guitar rock, electro, funk, and a whole range of musical genres, but on hearing them play that night I knew I just had to be in that band. They were super tight. I was drawn to the music, and seeing as they didn't have a drummer, I approached the singer and said to him, 'I love this music and you need a drummer.'

Then a new drum machine called the LinnDrum came out and it was a beast of technology that sounded great. The era of the drum machines was alive and well, and fast becoming the replacement of live drummers in the studios. It really did put a lot of drummers on the sideline for a while, but you can also play along with the drum machine, layering feels, and grooves on top of the kick and snare, which makes the drums sound as if there were two drummers.

The '80s were kicking with some awesome electro bands ruling the airwaves. *Human League*, *Utravox*, *Depeche Mode*, just to name a few. The big rock bands of the '70s lost members, mainly drummers, due to booze and drugs. R.I.P. John Bonham and Keith Moon. It must be hard when you get to super group status and you have a taste for drink and drugs. Sadly, Keith and John Bonham overindulged, and left this planet way too early. Most musicians never make it to the dizzying heights of success in the music business. I on the other hand never wanted to be a rock star, my only goal was to see the world from behind a drum kit and see how far I could go with it. Deep down I always lacked some confidence, not drive, I think the negativity from my mother regarding my choice of career always made me second guess if I had the talent and ability to work full-time in my dream job.

The year was 1983. The leader of this duo I saw in the Hakoah Club was a man called Ken Davis. During his break I asked him if I could audition, if I could try out for the band. He told me that if I wanted to join the band, I needed to buy a Simmons electronic drum kit. The Simmons drums had this huge digital sound. Every drummer from *Spandau Ballet* to *Van Halen* used them. It was the sound of the day. The work was there if I could buy one of these kits, so I approached my parents to back me for the two thousand dollar loan that I needed to buy the Simmons electronic drum kit. My parents said no, but I somehow managed to get a loan from a credit union and as soon as I got the two thousand dollars, I bought the electronic drum kit.

Ken Davis was a really driven guy who knew what he wanted, and he was a worker, a visionary and motivated person who didn't waste time. He quickly proceeded to assemble a full band. I dropped out of Horticulture College, which I was a year and a half into, left my job, and was now finally on my way to earning my living from playing drums. I dreamt big and the Lord provided, not that I was into religion at this stage of my life, but I was now officially earning my living from playing drums.

We rehearsed cover songs for two weeks at this house near Bondi Junction and then headed to the Gold Coast in sunny Queensland to play a month's residency at a place called The Resort. Ken then told me that there was one other thing that I needed to do as well. I had to practice six out of the seven days for two hours along with the drum machine. Ken would meet me in the auditorium after lunch each day and fire up the LinnDrum. I had to play along, keeping in sync, playing a beat he called the 'Doof Dah', this was his name for the kick and snare beat.

I asked him, 'What else do you want me to practice?'

He said, 'Nothing'.

I was a bit dumbfounded, as I thought that surely, he would want me to practice other drum rudiments or exercises, learn some songs perhaps, but no. It was my 'Wax on, Wax off' training. I didn't realise, but those hours each day playing along with the drum machine taught me a lot. It can get to be quite tiring and monotonous just playing the same beat for two hours. I didn't realise it at the time, but it really helped me to get used to playing with a machine that never gets tired and keeps perfect time.

We played six nights a week and each day I would be back again in the auditorium to have my workouts with my new electronic friend, who did sound great. Of course, I was excited to be a fulltime musician, I had finally achieved that goal but deep inside there was a feeling that from a career perspective I was not content. I felt that there was more to me. I was not sure what that was just yet but I had a gut feeling that drumming was not going to be my final career.

As for my mental health, I had forgotten about my breakdown at 17, that seemed to be well behind me. Little did I know what was to follow in years to come, but for now the words mental and health were far removed from me. I had no episodes of mania or depression; life was great, and I was living my dream as a professional musician. I was never a songwriter, and even though my parents made me learn piano from the ages of 6 –11, the reality of my musicality was limited. I had no idea about song structure or composition, so I was always going to accompany the others in the bands I played in, but that didn't bother me at all. I had a great sense of rhythm, and I adored playing drums.

I also believe a man must know his own limitations and I was not deceiving myself about my skills. In the drumming world I knew I was nothing special, but I had good timing and could play well along with a click track. I was a meat 'n' potatoes kind of player, and I just loved to play, whether it was practice, a gig, or recording in the studio. For me, it was never about being famous or making millions from a band. I just wanted to do my best to see how far I could go.

After the residency at The Resort ended, we went out on the road and toured for about seven months consistently. That band slowly drifted apart, the other guys wanted to do their own projects, and we broke up. I was back to checking the 'drummer wanted' ads around the rehearsal studios and music rags. Ken never stopped recording new material, he was always in the studio, and he always had me come in and lay down some drum tracks for him. He would also busk in the city on weekends and those busking days were a lot of fun. Ken would always have me come and join him when he busked, and we played in busy locations around the city. Every weekend, we would busk down at Circular Quay, or outside the Sydney Opera House. When we started busking, Ken sold tapes during the breaks to the people passing by. He had a lot of drive and energy, continually writing new material.

New technology arrived and his music was now available on the latest media format which was the Compact Disc (CD). Ken then forged a path into relaxation and meditation music. He was one of the few musicians I knew who circumvented the recording business, doing it all himself. By the time CDs really started to catch on, Ken had an impressive catalogue. Well over 20 albums. Meanwhile, I was auditioning for lots of bands. I finally landed a great part-time job in a great drum shop in the city called Andy Evans Drumcraft. I loved being in that shop surrounded by drum kits, cymbals and percussion instruments. I also took some lessons from Andy the owner who was a well-known Sydney Session Drummer.

One day while I was hanging around the rehearsal studios I used to practice at, I saw a notice on the pin board where bands would write up and place ads if they were looking for members. I took the number down and when I got home, rang up to audition for that gig. The keyboard player was a man I had watched play several times before at a venue called The Musician's Club, where he had a residency every Friday night. Leon Berger was originally from Russia and was a very proficient musician. He had studied at the Moscow Conservatory of Music. Leon was a great singer/ songwriter, and keyboard player. I auditioned for Leon's band and I remember being nervous, but I was called back a second time and I got offered the gig. This was huge. I could not believe my lucky break.

Leon immigrated to Australia in the mid '70s. Of course, back then he had to comply with the rules of communist Russia, but that didn't stop him from being a huge success. I was over the moon. Apart from being in this band there were other benefits that came along as well. Leon hired me for all the other sessions he recorded and produced for other people, and I was always paid well for my time. He was a perfectionist and knew exactly what he wanted in the studio. It was very intimidating, but at the end of the day, he knew what sounded good and was a great guy to work with and learn from. He also had a great sense of humour; it was challenging but fun at the same time.

Leon was a workaholic; he could spend days in the studio writing songs and recording them. One day, he rang me up and asked me if I wanted to play on a demo for a song with a new singer Tina Cross. Tina was a big star in New Zealand, and I was asked to come and play at EMI's studio 301 in Sydney. This song was the start of my musical journey for the next few years and provided me with my own 15 minutes of fame. The band was *Koo Dé Tah*. We recorded our debut single in January of '84 and it was released in April that year. The song didn't do much on the charts when it was first released.

While we were recording in Studio A, across the floor in Studio B, was another band called *Kids in the Kitchen*. They were being produced by Molly Meldrum. Molly, a legend of the Australian music industry was a friendly guy, not snobby at all. I will never forget seeing the guys from *Kids in the Kitchen* signing what seemed to be an endless line of photos for their fans. The photos must have gone 12 metres down the corridor between Studio B and Studio A. Right at that moment we were taking a break when Molly Meldrum walked out from Studio B. Leon knew Molly well, and I was honoured to meet this legend of the music industry. Molly was the brains behind a TV show called *Countdown* which was the music show back in the day. Everyone loved that show. Leon had been on the show a couple of times already and they shared a mutual respect. Leon invited Molly into Studio A to have a listen to the two tracks we had recorded. After he heard the songs, Molly invited us to go on the show. My excitement was through the roof, and I had butterflies already flapping in my stomach as soon as I got the good news.

Our studio line up for recording the album was Leon Berger, who wrote all the songs and played keyboard, Tina Cross our singer, John Bettison on guitar, and myself. About two weeks later the date was set, 4 August 1985, we were locked in to perform on the show. It was not my first time on TV as I'd done some TV work with Ken Davis before, but this show was an institution. It was also a great platform for Australian bands and artists. Each week, *Countdown* had guest presenters who would introduce international and local artists that appeared on the show. This was our break and when the single was released, it went to number three on the charts. It was a very exciting period to say the least.

Apart from working in the drum shop part-time, I had another great part-time job as a glorified dishwasher for a catering company that would cook and feed international touring bands. I loved that job, because it would give me an opportunity to work behind the scenes and see the backstage machinations of the rock industry. I was a mere kitchen hand, but being right in the thick of it, I got to see the road crew load in tonnes of equipment and rig the whole production together. First, we would feed the road crew their breakfast, then lunch. Once I had cleared up the plates and washed the pots, I had the golden pass which allowed me to be anywhere in the auditorium.

Then, the band would arrive at the arena at about 4 pm to do a sound check. I would think to myself that one day I was also going get to this level. Well, that was the dream, nothing wrong with dreaming big, right? On many occasions I befriended members of the crew and the musicians. One of my other jobs was to prepare the drinks in each of the stars' dressing rooms. I would place ice into the large plastic tubs and fill them with whatever the stars had on their specific rider list. Six bottles of Evian, six bottles of CocaCola, a bottle of whisky, one litre of fresh orange juice... Whatever they wanted to eat or drink in their dressing room, I had to put this together prior to them being in the building. After the sound check, the band would then sit for their dinner. I would work fast so I could be ready for when the band went on stage. My work was officially over, and I had the choice to be anywhere to enjoy the show. It was the best, I got to see so many great international acts, and I was being paid for the privilege!

During the last week in July '85, I was thrilled to do my glorified dishwashing job for the catering company. The band we were looking after was *Tears for Fears*. They sold out three shows at *Sydney Entertainment Centre*. They had an international number one hit with *Everybody Wants to Rule the World*. The band's drummer, Manny Elias and I became friends. I showed him around Sydney during that week, Manny was a friendly and down-to-earth guy, no rock star ego bullshit. He also happened to be Peter Gabriel's drummer. We went out on the following Friday and Saturday nights, and I asked him what he was doing for the rest of the tour, and *Tears for Fears* night. I also asked him what he was doing on the weekend. He said he was going down to Melbourne to be on *Countdown*, and I said 'Hey! I am going down to be on the show as well!'

Roland Orzabal and Curt Smith, the two songwriters of *Tears for Fears* were hosting the show. *Countdown* was filmed in front of a live studio audience. We didn't play live, but the audience was packed into the studio, and they were enthusiastic. The set director had placed me on the other side of the studio away from the rest of the band. There was a small group of audience members in front of me. While I was miming along to our song during that live-to-air (mime) performance, I looked up at one stage and at the back of the crowd right in front of me, there was Manny and Roland standing and giving me a big thumbs up. It was the best. For the first and probably only time in my life, I felt like a rock star. While nothing really beats playing a great gig in front of a live audience, I have to say, in that moment seeing those real rock stars acknowledge the dishwashing drummer was solid gold.

Between working with Leon and *Koo Dé Tah*, I also managed to get a national tour with Robyn Archer. I was 21, the baby in the group of hired guns, flying around the country playing the best venues in Australia. We played *Perth Concert Hall*, *QPAC Concert Hall* in Brisbane, *The Princess Theatre* and *Palais Theatre* in Melbourne, *Sydney Opera House*, *Festival Theatre* in Adelaide, some 500-seater in Alice Springs, and the *Wrest Point Hotel Casino* in Hobart, Tasmania.

Once a drummer or musician doesn't have to lug and set up their equipment, you have reached a level of touring that is hard to beat. You walk into the venue that you're going to play later that night and run a sound check with the band so everyone can make sure that they're happy with the stage sound. This would usually take an hour or so and then you would be on a break until showtime. Now it was my turn to be in the touring band and enjoy the free drinks prior to the show. We always had a few pre-show drinks to calm the nerves. After the show, it was usually more drinks, and an invite out somewhere, then back to your hotel room, sleep, then off to the next town for another gig. I loved the touring lifestyle; I was finally living my rock and roll dream!

The years 1984 and '85 were great for me. My music career just seemed to be flowing, I was getting work on other projects as well and I was continually touring, meeting some great musicians, and playing a lot of gigs from one end of Australia to the other. In the beginning of 1985, we went back into the studio to record the rest of the album. We were in there for about three months. I loved it. Sadly, we never got to head overseas. This was a disappointment, but our management and record company just couldn't make it happen. The record company only signed Tina and Leon to the recording contract. I was just a gun for hire, but I loved it, that didn't bother me at all. It was a bit like the *Eurythmics*. I was in the band and got paid well to be on call to come into the studio to record and when we went out on the road for three months at a time playing six nights a week.

That album we recorded had a classic '80s electropop sound, it should have done a lot better than it did. We released four singles with video clips and toured for about two years. Eventually I could see the slow death of the band falling apart and I think we were done. It was a gunslinger in a Western that had been shot several times but refused to die, and just like that, I was a drummer for hire again with no band to play with. I was at a real crossroad and only 23 years old.

Not too long after the band officially ended, I was looking around for another band to join when I was offered a job in sales for a computer games company. The owner of this business, Akiva, said, 'Come on you can do this.'

I knew in my heart that I could always do something else, even though I was never sure of what that something really was. I was also getting serious with my girlfriend who came from a family that I knew would not be happy if their daughter married a drummer. So, after a lot of serious thought, I decided to take up Akiva's offer. I knew it meant the end of my career as a drummer. I had toured around Australia three times during the last few years, and I was a bit over it. If I was serious about still being a drummer, I would have to leave Australia and find a band either in LA or London. My heart was with my girlfriend, and I didn't want to leave her, so I thought to myself, how bad can it be selling computer games? Akiva seemed to think I had what it takes, so a week or so later I began my career in sales.

Working for Akiva was an incredible experience. He was and still is a great mentor to me, and he taught me a lot about selling. While he was the managing director of the business, he would still close some of the biggest sales. I couldn't do what he did and was in awe of the sales he would pull off with some major chains such as Kmart. Every Friday, the sales figures were collated by state, and he would make comments beside the results. The comments were mostly encouraging, but if the sales were lacking or there was room for improvement, he would let me know. Naturally I wanted to sell as much as I could, and I did achieve my sales targets most of the time. If I didn't, Akiva knew how to motivate me, and I was encouraged to dig deep and do my best. When I did well, his positive comments made my day.

I really loved selling, and it was a fun industry to be working in. There were a few weeks when I really did crush my sales targets, thinking this week I know I am going to impress Akiva when he sees the sales numbers. Well, on this particular week, the Friday report was handed out. My figures were fantastic, and his sales blew me out of the park. I looked at the sales sheet, and yet again Akiva, had done a massive order with Kmart, dwarfing my sales. He was next level, both with his sales and his business acumen. Nonetheless, I loved working in his company, it gave me a start in a new industry, with a whole new career path into my first corporate sales job.

CHAPTER 15
What's It Like Being Manic?

What is it really like to be manic? There are those that are friends or relatives of the person who is manic that I know would disagree with this, but people with bipolar one mania would gladly take this part of the condition over the deep depression on the flip side.

Here are some signs of manic behaviour:

1. Spending money like it's never going to end

2. Overactive sexual urges

3. Irritable feelings, not being able to relax

4. Lack of sleep – this is a big one

5. Arguing with friends and family

6. Flourish of ideas that are overwhelmingly positive to you but nobody else

7. Psychotic episodes, hearing voices

8. Increased use of recreational drugs and alcohol

9. Pressured speech

10. Grandiosity 11. Impulsive behaviour

12. Cannot sit or be still.

Mania is caused by a chemical imbalance in the brain. To put it simply, the brain is flooded with feel-good chemicals. It's like being high on cocaine, the uplift in mood can be very hard to contain. Without an increase of meds to help bring it under control and slow the brain down, the mania can run for days, weeks and even months. Before I accepted that I have bipolar, I was like a dog off the leash.

When manic I always have racing thoughts and ideas, and in the beginning, I feel great. The racing thoughts and increase in energy makes it hard to sleep. These days, included in my daily medication is an antipsychotic that helps me get to sleep. When I'm not elevated, I take 100mg of this medication and that's enough of a dose to send me off to sleep. When elevated, I need to take between 400 to 600mgs minimum, sometimes even more. Without any medication, I can easily go up to three days without sleep which is obviously not good as I build up a sleep debt. When not elevated I don't like sleeping during the day but once I am aware that I'm manic, I may need to take 100 to 200mgs of this medication during the day to reel in the mania. This is the responsible thing to do. Mania causes a restlessness or agitation which is a horrible feeling, and this medication helps take that feeling away.

The feeling of onset mania creeps in very slowly, it's so sneaky that it can be very hard to notice that the manic elevation has begun. Suddenly, you're feeling good and unaware of the fact that your brain has begun spinning faster. I seem to talk louder with my friends, they notice that they can't get a word in and if they do, I will finish their sentences. My energy level is through the roof. If I am listening to music, I want it turned up loud, if I'm playing my guitar, I want to crank that up as well. I have ridiculous amounts of energy and the hardest thing is to work out how to burn it off. The racing thoughts that enter my mind can lead to bad behaviour in the blink of an eye. I could easily crave a drink or want to get high, my driving becomes reckless, and if people on the roads drive badly, cutting me off or pulling bad turns in front of me, this can quickly lead to road rage.

It's taken me a long time to understand the feeling of onset mania. Twenty six years since my first psychotic mania, I'm now very much aware when my mood begins to lift, and I take it very seriously. Now I know that I need to stay at home, I have learnt that this is the safest place to be. Being manic around other people is difficult. I can be a handful with this increase in energy. While my behaviour can be hard for others to deal with, it's something that's beyond my control. That is why I have learnt to just stay in my safe place at home until it blows over. This can take several weeks. Naturally I would love to be out at night or doing more things during the day, but with the massive increase of my slow-down meds, I can't drive or use a chainsaw, and certainly not combine both of those activities at the same time. Once the right number of meds are on board, it's only a matter of about 40-50 minutes, then suddenly, my brain blacks out. Many times, I have woken up to my surprise hours later in a sitting position on the couch in front of the TV or sitting at my desk. This is not ideal but at least I have managed to get a few hours of sleep in.

I have also identified that my manias come on every spring and sometimes it can also arrive as summer ends going into autumn, but not all people with bipolar are affected by the change of seasons. In spring, the bears come out of hibernation, the flowers are blooming, nature is alive and well. The bipolar type one's are also coming alive, and if they are not on top of their meds, will end up in the psych ward. I remember one spring I had the good sense to ring the hospital to check how much medication I needed to take. The nurse in the psych ward was impressed that I had the common sense to call. I asked why she was so surprised, she told me that the ward was full of people who were manic, so she congratulated me for being responsible.

In the past when I was either in denial or not taking my meds as per my doctor's instructions, the manias have got the better of me. I have been triggered and once that happens, I find it hard to wind down. If I don't take this seriously, I'm gambling with my health. It took me a long time to apply the discipline of staying home, but it must be done, otherwise things can turn pearshaped in no time. As mentioned, I up the dose of antipsychotic meds, but there is no fixed amount as to how much I need to take. The goal is to get to sleep. From about 6 pm I start my evening med regime; I keep taking more every two hours until I drop. This is the only way to help wind down the manic elevation.

One of the worst things about that medication is that it opens the 'secret hidden seven chambers of the stomach'. During these periods, it's easy to intend on having a healthy diet but because my guard is down, I just can't stop eating. This is the worst side effect. I can't seem to control myself and go nuts with whatever food is in the fridge. I wish I didn't get these cravings to eat but my mind is in a fog and my stomach does the thinking. Over a two-week mania I could easily put on 10 kilograms if I am not careful. I don't like the weight gain, but I will take that over being out of control and locked up in the laughing academy. If I happen to wake for some reason, I take a sleepwalk into the kitchen. From there on, it's a blur of hands and food. I am not sure why that medication makes me so hungry, but not taking them is just going to make the mania last longer, so I accept it as part of the healing process.

If I don't follow a strict plan for recovery when manic, I know where I can end up. I am no longer in denial about my condition, and I take it very seriously. I can look back and have the wisdom from past manic episodes and be able to tell these stories with some humour, but at the time it was no joke. Everything can be great with hindsight. I look back and ask myself, 'Why did those past manias get to the point of those interventions?' I can only say that in the past when I was manic, I was out of control. Once elevated, it doesn't take much for me to be pushed to a more out of control state of mania. Most of the time it is usually people who push my buttons and I go off. My concerned family simply don't know what to do, so they call the Community Health Team who in turn come with police to evaluate the situation. Once they arrive to evaluate me, if I come across elevated to them then I get taken away in the back of a police paddy wagon. I have had some people around me say that they know other people with bipolar and those people do not behave in the same way as me. They control their condition better. Well not all bipolar is the same, and of course looking back I wish I had not behaved the way I did. I was not well, and my judgement was way off. I am not making excuses; it is just the way it went down.

There are two distinct types of bipolar, type one and type two. As someone with type one, the more extreme form, I get mania, hypomania, psychosis (which only happened during my first mania), and on the other side, severe depression. There are some common threads between BP1 and BP2, but from what I know about type two, they do not get the crazy increase of energy. Eventually the increase in meds start to work, and my mood begins to come down. I know because the increase in medication puts me to sleep faster and for a longer period. This is good because I can finally pay back my sleep debt. The wind down can take up to five weeks or so. It is not a sudden thing that just snaps back overnight just because I have increased my meds. Bringing my brain down to a normal level is not easy. It is very hard to be at home when I'm manic, but these days I have enough sense to stop myself from going out. It has taken a long time to apply this discipline. In the past, if I did go out, that meant drinking and taking drugs, primarily cocaine. I can't justify it by saying anything other than I have had drug and alcohol issues since my late teens. I could investigate reasons why, and I could blame it on several things. Growing up as a keen surfer, pot was big in surf culture back then, and in the Eastern Suburbs of Sydney where I grew up, binge drinking, and the drug culture was deemed 'cool'. It didn't help that it was also glorified in movies, and my favourite comic books the *The Fabulous Furry Freak Brothers*.

When I didn't have my manic filter turned on, I would want to take the manic up another notch by self-medicating. Naturally this is the opposite of what I needed to do. I have no idea why I had the craving to get higher. As for the lack of self-control, I can only put this down to a lack of understanding and insight into my manic state of mind. Of course, I also know I'm just not thinking right, and I am in lift-off mode, running with the mania as opposed to putting the brakes on to slow it down. Now, when the mania hits, I place myself into lockdown. I only go out to do the shopping, preferably at nighttime when there are not many people around and the parking is easy.

As mentioned, when I am elevated, I am easily angered or aggravated. I am already in a state of heightened awareness, so it doesn't take much for me to blow up. I would like to think that I have now learnt to control my anger and when a mania has blown in, I'm responsible with handling the mood. Going back a few years now, I had the blow up of all blow ups with a manic episode that ended up causing terrible emotional pain with some relatives and a few of my closest friends. I have learnt from past manias, but this elevation was the one that taught me the most and made me realise that if I am manic, I am best off just to avoid people and lay low until the manic wind has blown out from my sails. I just cannot be out when I am elevated.

When my brain has lit up with mania it is hard to control my emotions. I can be triggered so easily. It is not easy following the stay-at-home rule, but that is what must be done, no ifs, buts, or maybes. When manic, I refuse to listen to anyone. In the past that held true, but today I do listen to the people that care, and especially to my psychiatrist. It took about two to three years for me to accept that I have bipolar. Living in denial and putting my head in the sand seemed so much easier. Then it probably took me another 20 years to get to really understand that every year I get elevated, and when I am, it's just best to lay low and dope myself up to my eyeballs with the right meds, avoid the selfmedication, and wait until it blows over. I never want to be that frightening manic out in public, or at home. Best to just bounce off the walls at home, and once I take the right number of meds, I'm just going to be winding myself into the lounge and off to sleep for a few weeks.

CHAPTER 16
Winding The Mania Down

As mentioned, at the start of a manic episode I would have lost at least one or two nights of sleep, so that is a sleep debt of about sixteen hours. The meds take time to work. Taking the extra meds is not an instant panacea. The longer I let the mania run, the longer it is going to take for me to get better.

Don't be fooled by thinking that you can come back to a level playing field without bringing your sleep into a healthy pattern. Sleep is the most important measure for me, when I notice that my sleep is increasing, I know I am beginning to come back down to earth. The manic mind can be a cruel instrument and if not respected, I know I am going to just prolong what needs to be done eventually. The increase in meds does its work over the next few weeks. I follow doctor's orders and while it sometimes may be hard to do, I know it is the only way I can come back into a healthy mind space.

Some nights, it's a real conflict of emotions, I really do want to stay up and just do anything other than sleep. But I have learnt over the years that taking the increase in meds as per my doctor's instructions is the only way that I am going to calm down the tornado in my brain. I try to enjoy the creative energy as much as possible, and if I am not feeling too agitated, I can get by during the day without having to take something to take the edge off. But come early evening, I need to start the nighttime regime.

I know that I have some close friends and family who keep an eye on me. They know when I am off and running and get on my case big time, I have no choice but to comply. So, I take my meds and, in the morning, have my friends, 'the sleep police' check in. They ask, 'so how many hours did you sleep last night?' Anything over six hours is fantastic. Yes, I am lucky that I have these few that care, nobody wants to see me lose the plot or end up in a world of pain in the laughing academy. Best to do the wind down routine at home in my environment. For that I am grateful. Then there is my psych doc who keeps an even tighter vigil on me. When things are well, I may have a session with him every 4–6 weeks. When I am elevated, he wants to check in every 2–3 days. He is a good man, and I am lucky that he cares.

When manic, life is looking so good, there is not a negative thought in my mind. Ideas are popping and I feel like I cannot fail. When the meds start to work, they do numb the creativity and take away the energy that is pushing me along at a million miles an hour. Sometimes it can be hard to determine the good ideas from the bad ones. But for now, it's not about ideas, it's all about the controlled slow down. And as things begin to slow down, so to do the rush of ideas. It is always better to have a soft landing with none of the nasty leftovers that mania can cause.

Over the next few weeks, I am getting more sleep hours in. There is still creativity and if I am lucky, I can determine the good ideas from the elevated crazy ones. Some ideas become clearer, some just get parked or put into the 'forget about it' folder of crazy dreams. Others, well they are dreams that remain just that, and all I can say about that is, how boring would life be without dreams! If only this manic energy could be funnelled off to the depressive side of the condition when you so desperately need a boost to bring you back into balance. Sadly, that's not how it works, and that I suppose is the cruelty of this condition. When you're up or manic, you just feel almost invincible. When you're on the slide down into depression, your energy is nowhere to be found, and avoiding a downward spiral into depression is now the priority, steering clear of the darkness is now the one thing to avoid.

CHAPTER 17
What Goes Up...

The crash, once it comes can be devastating. There may be some warning or self-awareness that the mania has ended, and at this point I need to assess my feelings, asking myself where I am on my bipolar mood scale. If I was a plus 4 out of 5 on the manic side, sliding down to a minus 2 out of 5 on the depression side can happen quickly.

As we all know, what goes up must come down, and before I know it, I can become engulfed by the heavy blanket of depression. First comes the realisation that I have descended off cloud mania. It's an awareness that the mania has stopped. Suddenly, the sunny days begin to disappear, and big rain clouds have closed in from nowhere, it's starting to hail and get cold. I look around and think, *where did this come from? How have things changed so quickly?* The only thing to do is to run for cover, but there is nowhere to run to, I'm about to get wet, but hopefully not soaked. The bipolar pendulum has now definitely swung in the opposite direction, and there is nothing I can do except be aware of what might follow.

The mania that has powered on for the past period with so many ideas, and full-on energy, has drained the battery. It is only once the gas runs out of the tank that these ideas and manic thoughts of my (possibly) distorted reality can become the land of broken dreams, pain, and suffering. Indeed, it can all come down around me like a house of cards. I can go from being elevated and then headfirst into a depressed state if I am not careful. Although I am aware that I'm heading into this horrible space, there is nothing I can do about it. I find myself trapped, holding no more than a garden hose to extinguish the raging flames of depression.

Last year I had an elevation, I was very proud of how I conducted myself during it. No conflicts, not one person upset me or pushed my buttons, and I certainly didn't piss off anyone else (I think). I became elevated at the end of February 2022, and my psych doctor got my medication levels sorted. One medication that I thought he was going to keep the same, he asked me to increase. I asked him why he wanted me to take more of that medication, and he said that he didn't want me to fall into a depression after the mania. I thought to myself that surely, I am not going to end up back in the land of pain and suffering. I'm feeling good, yes, a little too good, but depression? No way!

Well, let's just say I had some financial ducks lined up in a row. As I moved through mid to end of March, I could see that those little duckies just may not come to fruition. By the beginning of the first week in April, I could see that these business deals were melting away faster than a Paddle Pop in the sun. I was really counting on that business to come in. I needed the money, and as those deals went south, so did my mood; I was sinking. Within a short space of time, I was in the quicksand of depression, and I was going down faster and faster. I could not believe what was happening, and there was nothing that I could do about it. As for my old friend, my depression, it was the quicksand, and it was sticky. I was beginning to feel helpless, and as it surrounded me, the safe, happy land was out of reach, I was in trouble and there was not a thing I could do about it. I felt helpless, I was stuck, and here we go again…

As the fantastic mood of the mania was enjoyed for a brief period, it was followed by a few weeks of home detention with copious amounts of meds, the feel good turned into a euthymic state after a few weeks and then boom. I was in the pit of depression, and I could not believe it. I hated it. I felt paralysed. Beating this force of negative energy was going to once again take time and the right mindset. I was not prepared to get myself out from the darkness just yet. I had a fair bit of self-evaluation and mental bashing to go through first. That and a lot of mindless couch time.

Accepting the fact that I had now slid into this mental funk was a given, getting out of the quicksand of depression was another thing. There are millions of people around the world that would agree with me that it is the worst a person can feel, and it is just about the hardest thing a person can do to turn it around.

A few weeks went by, and I think I finally got bored of feeling sorry for myself and being bored out of my mind. I also knew the one thing that was going to help me were the small steps out from that horrible place. My psychiatrist did not prescribe me any antidepressants. I have not done well on them in the past. I am not saying that they are not good, I just find that for me, the one thing that works is to break out of the depression one small step at a time. First, I must get out of bed; lying in bed and waking to another day of depression is the worst. The hardest thing is getting out of the house and going for a walk. It is not easy to do this simple task but if I can get myself moving and can manage to make this a daily task then I can push myself to eventually go twice a day. From there, I push myself to do some other tasks and then eventually my mind does turn around. It's as if suddenly, I spring back into a better headspace, and I am feeling much better.

I don't want to make this sound easy as it is not. But after having gone through so many depressions and clawing my way back, I know myself and what I need to do. For some reason it seemed easier this time. It is never easy, it is always a challenge against my worst enemy, myself. I find I just get to a point where I have had enough, and in the past, it has taken longer, months, and months. I think this time was rather fast. Within four weeks I was feeling a lot better and back to doing more.

I know if I didn't set myself up mentally with the small goals of say, a walk followed by shopping for groceries, then hopefully the gym, then I can get down to doing other things that give me pleasure such as playing music. Finally, my concentration comes back, and I can read a book or write. It is also something that I need to maintain, or I will quickly slide back into the negative headspace and become my worst enemy again.

Why be hard on myself? There is no reason to be cruel, but I know I can be, and it is such a waste of emotion. Thinking positively takes effort but I need to do this and work at it constantly. If I don't, then I know where I am going to end up, back to being a negative, unhappy person. So, if you are feeling flat, make small plans for the next day. Baby steps are the only way I have been able to come out of my funk, and I know this can work for you as well.

CHAPTER 18
Locked Ward Round Two

Remember that suicide attempt and waking up to my liquid charcoal breakfast? Apart from the free gourmet meal, I was now back behind bars in the laughing academy feeling like a total loser for a failed suicide attempt. I was now in an extremely dark place. Don't get me wrong, they had wonderful fluorescent lights and that familiar courtyard I had legally been freed from previously. But this time I was a shell of a man. If I thought that I was depressed before the suicide attempt, now I was well and truly in the darkest of mental holes a person could possibly find themselves in with no answers for anything.

The voice of my psychosis was nowhere to be heard, and I was in the locked ward with the same mixed bag of schizophrenic, bipolar and chronically depressed individuals. I was given some mood stabilisers along with antidepressants, but deep in the grey matter, I was lost. This feeling of loss and despair with no roadmap or shining beacon to guide me out was a compounding feeling that was being fed by yours truly. It's what we do. We love to beat ourselves up and treat oneself with the worst mental beating. It is a continual dressing down, a self-imposed punishment. If we spoke to others the way our internal dialogue speaks to us sometimes, we might be arrested for verbal assault.

On top of the lowest mood ever achieved by mankind, I had blown all my money, and could not even think straight. Forget about business plans, I had no plans whatsoever. Of course, I had to ask the treating doctors how long they were going to keep me here, and from memory there was the obligatory, 'You will
be released when you are better.'

This time there was not going to be any magistrates hearing, not that I could afford a lawyer. In my condition, I was totally defeated. I also had a small issue, I had to accept the doctor's diagnosis and it was one of the hardest things to accept. I was curious about treatment options, so I asked one of the doctors, 'What if the antidepressants don't work, what's the next possible treatment?'

The doctor said, 'If the medications don't work, we can try ECT.'

What? 'What is ECT?'

He explained the procedure to me. I was shocked, no pun intended there. I thought to myself, *I have got to get better. There is no way I want to go through that*. No rubber mouthguard and electricity to bring me out of this depression. *NO F-ing WAY!* The thought of that kept going over and over in my mind. I started thinking that I was going to have to try and get out of this depressed state with the medication and some other method, anything, just please don't put me on the slab and shock me back to my former self. I believe it is a popular technique for severely depressed, and I am in no way mocking this technique as it obviously has proven results for people with severe depression. But the thought of this technique freaked me out.

Am I in a remake of *One Flew Over the Cuckoo's Nest*? Was there going to be some other method of healing that was going to freak me out? I was walking the wards, eating the hospital food with no release date in site. I knew I was also on some kind of suicide watch, but I had no desire to take my life or try anything like that again, I was grateful in one way to be alive, albeit I felt like a loser. But the reality is, G-d gave me a second chance, and for that I am forever grateful.

But the road to being happy again was nowhere in sight. I felt I was more lost than the Israelites in the desert following Moses. Well at least he had a cloud to follow, all I had were the clouds of depression that had settled in my mind. Depression is a bitch, and I had no idea that this was not going to be my last dance with the devil in the dark room of my mind, but it was my first walk with the black dog, as Winston Churchill liked to call it. Winston Churchill had bipolar, and he ran a country in the worst era that Britain experienced. How on earth did he cope with his dark days? Whiskey, I think, but was he a type one or type two? I never found out.

How do you come back from this darkness? Good question. Right then and there in that ward, my second time, I would begin the rebuild. I realised I just had to wade through this mental mud and get out of the quicksand of depression. I could not even see the dry land from where I was standing, but apparently it was there somewhere and if I kept following the programme of meds, and just being, then I would somehow get to my yellow brick road. Sadly, they could not have just replaced my defective brain with a new fully functioning one. I also heard that there was no stem cell programme or even a software programme upgrade for what I had. Apparently, I had to do my own software upgrade and I had no idea how long that was going to take.

CHAPTER 19
Deep In The Pit Circa 1996

Weeks had passed by in the laughing academy and my treating doctors finally gave me the all-clear to be released. My girlfriend and I moved into my grandmothers old flat. I was lucky enough to have this place for us to move to. The flat was a 170 metre walk to Bondi Beach, which is a great location, provided you can get out of the flat to enjoy the beach.

I don't know how I passed the exit exam because I was still in a deep depression, I couldn't face the world outside and the world in my head was spinning the same stories. *How did things get so bad? How was my judgement so off?* As for being social, there were one or two people that I could face, and they could tell I was broken. I felt shame and embarrassment, so the last thing I wanted was to bump into people. During this time, I locked myself in that flat feeling sorry for myself, only heading out with my girlfriend to do some grocery shopping. I couldn't enjoy listening to music, and just wanted to lie in bed all day. Sticky Fingers came over to visit me, I had been home for a few weeks already and he saw that I hadn't even assembled my stereo. He said, 'Come on, let's do it together,' so we plugged it all in. He then said, 'Don't worry about the money you owe me. You didn't rip me off, you were unwell. So, forget about it.' It was a huge relief, at least that was one less thing to think about.

I will never forget one time when I was out, and I bumped into someone I knew. They said, 'Hey, I haven't seen you in ages, have you been away?'

I said, 'Yeah, I have been away.' He obviously didn't hear about where I went away to and in my mind, I was happy to keep the location of my vacation a secret. I had been away alright. Away in the black halls of depression hell. This was my first real bipolar depression. There were no more voices telling me this or that, no more prophecy, there was just the one sad voice in my head playing like a broken record. I was hopelessly depressed and feeling sorry for myself. If only I had done this or that, things would not have gone out of control. I would like to believe this but as I was to learn later, getting sick was no coincidence. Apparently, Jews don't believe in that. We believe good or bad, everything happens for a reason, sometimes the reason is not clear for us, and a lot of the time it will never make sense, but we just have to accept and push on.

I would need the time to bring myself back from that dark place so I could face the world and society in general. The only way out is to be good to yourself, stop the negative thinking, this is so hard to do but certainly not impossible. Thinking a bit about the past is okay, but then clear that thought. I will say it is okay to look back a bit and reflect on a mistake, but to dwell on this just drives me mad, and it's not healthy. We can't change the past as we know, so why dwell on it? Give yourself a break. Create some activities and if you can, be in the company of others. And I know this is a lot easier said than done.

CHAPTER 20
The Story Of The Watch

The year was 1995. I had a roof over my head and was lucky that my girlfriend was still with me. I was still licking my mental wounds, but I had at least been going down to the beach on a regular basis for a walk and a swim. On this particular day, it was really overcast, and my girlfriend and I walked a couple of laps of the beach. The surf was big and messy, but I decided to go in for a bodysurf anyway. I was in the water for about 20 minutes, and I came out feeling a bit lighter, I felt something was not right and looked at my left arm only to see my watch had come off in the surf. I was beside myself. I went back out into the waves, but they were relentless. Wall after wall of white water was coming at me and I was diving to the bottom desperately trying to feel for my watch. I must have been in the surf for 30 minutes then I just gave up and in despair walked out from the ocean to the sand.

I told my girlfriend, naturally she could not say much except, 'Why did you wear the watch into the surf in the first place?' It was a TAG diver's watch, so it was water resistant to 150 metres. I'm sure it went right to the bottom, only about 10 metres and that was that. It was not the first watch I had lost in the surf at Bondi, but this watch had special meaning to me. Back when I started my first real business, I was importing computer components from Taiwan and Japan. On my first business trip I was looking at some watches in the duty-free section before heading to the departure gate. I saw this watch, rang my wife, and asked if I could buy it. It was fifteen hundred dollars, and I had the money, so she said, 'Why not? Treat yourself.'

The watch became the material symbol for my newfound success. So, from that point of view, it had some emotional value tied to it. On the other hand, it was the only material possession I had of any value. It was my Joab moment. I looked into the sky, and I said to G-d, 'I lost my house, my business my money and now the one thing I valued, from the last few years. Dear Lord, did you have to take my watch as well?'

Apparently, yes. I was so shattered. In the months ahead, I missed that darn watch. It was to be a big lesson; I knew I had grown up as so many in the Eastern Suburbs with our focus on the material. Now I really had been stripped of all my material possessions, it was time to take a new path from the material to the spiritual. I didn't plan on this but when you have loss in your life, especially health, we have so many questions to ask. But who can have the answers? Naturally, being Jewish I went to see a Rabbi. That was the start of my spiritual journey.

I'm not going to say I found G-d, I've always believed in G-d, I was just not raised in a religious environment. My parents grew up as religious, keeping kosher and observing the Sabbath, but after their nightmare going through the holocaust, like so many Jews they didn't continue these religious practices. My grandmother was the only one that kept a kosher home and I remember seeing her pray many times, mainly at night. My grandmother was a young woman during First World War, and then a mother with a son during Second World War. Her spirit was strong, and she did not doubt G-d; I admired her strength.

Meanwhile, my mum who always made sure we had our Friday night Shabbat meal, lost her parents and her sister, along with her sister's three-year-old son. So, I cannot blame her for losing faith. How does someone go through such horror and not be affected? We never kept a kosher home, and she would send me off to school with ham sandwiches. Actually, ham and cheese, which is a double whammy as kosher Jews do not mix meat and milk. To her, it didn't matter, and as for me I knew nothing about keeping kosher. If non-kosher food doesn't taste so bad, what was all the fuss in not eating it?

CHAPTER 21
Let's Get Spiritual

Why, Lord, did you have to take the one material possession I had left? I didn't get an answer from him, so I went to the Yeshiva Synagogue on Flood Street in Bondi to seek out a Rabbi for me to talk to. I found a wonderful man who I asked if he had some time to spare now as I had some questions for him.

We sat down, and I told him of my new mental status. I then told him how I lost everything including the watch. He told me that the watch was replaceable so I should not worry about that. Was it a lesson from above? Possibly. Was losing my mental health also a lesson from above? I asked him, because it was a brutal one, and I said, 'I am finding it hard to come to terms with my diagnosis.'

Then he said the following: 'In life we are always being challenged and G-d doesn't give you any challenge that you can't cope with or overcome. If you fall off a horse, you dust yourself off and get back on.'

I told him I don't ride a horse and he laughed saying, 'Well you know what I mean.' Then he told me to get 10 people together around a table and have them write down their problems, 'when we look at everyone else's problems we will always stick with our own and not swap.'

He then asked me something else. 'Have you put on *tefillin* today?' I said, 'I have never put on *tefillin*, and that includes today.'

He went to grab his and placed the box (attached to a leather strap) at the top of my arm, I had to repeat a blessing after him.

He then started to wind the leather strap around my arm and hand. Then he placed the other box on my head, and he asked me to repeat the words of another blessing. The laying of the *tefillin* was completed with the arm strap adjusted to now also be wrapped around my fingers. I then recited the *Shema* prayer. I did remember this from my basic Sunday school; this practice and *mitzvah* (good deed) is only practised by males. I asked him if I must do this every day. He said, 'No, on Saturdays you can have a day off.'

It felt strange, but this was a big deal apparently. I had no understanding of the value of this, but he told me that this action combines the heart and the mind with G-d.

Now I had some answers, and I had this new *mitzvah* which was going to help me spiritually. Most men start this at the age of 13 on their bar mitzvah. I must have got the message mixed up as I was 31, but they say it is never too late to start doing good deeds. Especially one as important as this. In the days that followed, I would go to the morning service, borrow a set of *tefillin* and have the Rabbi teach me again and again until I got the binding technique correct. As alien as this felt and looked, I would look around the synagogue and all the men were praying with their *tefillin* on. I knew some of the men, one was a doctor, others were successful businessmen, there were about 25 men all with the boxes on their arm and head, praying. These guys are not stupid, if they're all doing this there must be something special about it.

I read up on it, and I still found it a bit confusing and hard to grasp. When I enquired about buying one for myself, I was shocked at how expensive they were. A cheap set was seven hundred dollars, and they went up from there. In time I saved and managed to buy a good second-hand pair for four hundred dollars. I had my own holy boxes, and to this day I have continued to put them on six days a week.

Don't think I became religious; I like to think that I became more spiritually aware. I now see this act as part of my daily routine. It is my spiritual medication. I may have missed a day here and there if I was quite unwell, but now I can't imagine not doing it. Back then, a few of my friends had also begun their path as well. I admire those guys as they have been able to be more observant than me, but it is not a contest, and I have struggles just like everyone else.

The most important thing that came out of my visits to this Rabbi was the fact that he helped me to not worry about the material so much. If we have loss, we were meant to have loss. It is hard to accept, but that is a part of life. When it comes to health, well everyone has some kind of health issue. He really helped me to come to grips with the loss of my material possessions and told me to keep up with the *tefillin* and that will help me, even though it may be hard to see, it is a big deal for us Jewish men.

CHAPTER 22
Time To Get Back To Work

The time finally arrived when I started to feel good enough to start looking for work. I got tired of being home and watching hours of mindless, boring television. Remember the year was 1995, Netflix had not been created and the internet was in its infancy used only by geeks or the military.

I saw an ad in the paper for a sales job with Telecom New Zealand selling telco services. I went off to the recruitment company for an initial interview and the lady who interviewed me decided to put me forward. To say I was nervous was an understatement. I had not worked for a corporate in six years, and that environment is intimidating. The sales manager who interviewed me was like an army drill sergeant. Sergeant Tony was an old school tyrannical sales manager who was a good salesman in his own right. He sold me on this incredible future, about the internet and where it was heading. He told me that in the not-too-distant future you will be able to watch a football game and at the same time from the screen you would be able to somehow order a pizza online that would arrive just in time for your game. Yes, these types of services were coming, and that it was this division of Telecom New Zealand that was going to be selling these new internet based services. Who would have thought that only several years away we would all be using these apps to order food from our own handheld devices, along with other services for home delivery?

A few days later, the recruiter rang me and said that I had been offered the job. This division of TCNZ was called PacStar. There were seven salespeople in this sales team, each with their targeted industries to focus on. After some sacrifices they gave me two vertical markets to focus on which really were the dregs. Transport and travel were my hunting ground. It was now time to push myself every day to get dressed and get into work.

As for the sexy internet technology we were supposed to be selling, well none of that was on the menu, we were selling fax broadcasting. One good thing about the job was the building and location in the city. It was a Tier 1 building called Grosvenor Place, on George Street near Circular Quay, downtown. Six months later, PacStar moved to an even better office building next to the brand-new Sheraton On The Park Hotel. While most of the sales team was competitive, as salespeople are, I had now managed to befriend a fellow sales assassin DC. As we had sold the Sheraton On The Park Hotel next door a fax service for each room in the hotel, the boss also managed to get us cheap memberships to their gym. DC and I signed up and while field marshal Tuff Tony the sales manager demanded our lie sheets (sales prospects) and a rigorous oneon-one meeting each week, in addition to our group sales meetings, DC and I still managed to work out where to hide for a lunchtime refresher, after our one-hour long gym session.

You didn't think we were going to hit the gym before or after work? No way! Sales guys need flexibility like yogis need a mat. You can't force salespeople to achieve the results they need to obtain without flexibility. It is a challenging role with targets and KPI's. The usual pressure of being only as good as your last month's sales rang true in that office, and of course we were ranked by sales each month. Salespeople also need autonomy and the freedom to bring those results in. We doctored our sales prospects sheets that the boss wanted to go over in the one-on-one meetings. Sometimes a bit of poetic licence had to be applied because the boss was all over us. So long as our lie sheets looked good and you made sales, and hit or came close to your monthly targets, that was all that mattered.

I was now back at work for this telco giant with my own work cubicle in an open-plan office, and sometimes I just could not help but think back to a time not so long ago when I had my own business, and I was doing well. *How did that all come apart?* In these moments I would look back and that was a killer. I would be at the printer to print off material and just shake my head, I couldn't believe I was working for some corporate again, in what I would call *"slave to the rhythm"*. I think *The Who* put it best when they wrote the lyrics *"Meet the new boss, same as the old boss"*.

I hated it.

I found selling the fax broadcasting service so darn boring. For those that don't know what a fax machine is, you didn't miss much in the evolution of communications. It came and conquered for about eight years, then email changed the game forever. A fax machine can only send one page at a time. Fax broadcasting is when you send the same fax or message out to thousands of addresses very quickly. To be able to do this, you needed a million-dollar piece of hardware with the various lists of numbers loaded on it. The client would send their one or two pages to us, and we would broadcast their message out to thousands of fax machines anywhere in the world within minutes. Today, they probably exist somewhere in some form.

If you were a big enough company, we sold those fax broadcasting 'fridges' as well if you had a lazy million. I never sold one of those big fridge-looking machines, but my sales buddy DC did. He took me into the data centre of Telecom Italia who were setting up shop now that the Australian telecoms market was being deregulated. DC took me into this insane data centre, which I have to say was very cool. He showed me the machine, the size of a large fridge. He laughed and then told me they hadn't even hooked it up! It probably never got hooked up. I don't think Telecom Italia ever got off the ground in Australia either. We looked at this one-million-dollar piece of tech, which started depreciating by the minute. It was going down in value like ripening fruit. Not that I was feeling sorry for Telecom Italia, those big telcos had so much money, depreciating hardware was merely a line item on a balance sheet to them. We laughed and went to the gym, followed by a liquid lunch.

Today that machine might make a museum piece in some tech corner. Technology does march onward. Smaller, faster, and cheaper seems to be the trend of tech. Five years warranty is a lifetime for a piece of hardware, your laptop, your phone, your games console. They might say lifetime warranty, but don't get sucked into the hype, there is a new piece of kit coming soon.

Soon the wheels of our division began to fall off. 1996 was three quarters done and I felt as if I had stuck at it for about as long as I could take. I could see the writing on the wall for PacStar, so I started looking for something else and found a call back service. International phone calls were expensive back in 1995, but this callback service was a fraction of the price of an international call, and I had heard that a lot of people were making money from selling this service. I decided to give it a go even though it was commission only. I left TCNZ and ventured out on my own as an independent sales agent. Stupid move.

It wasn't easy. I found it incredibly hard to get clients. My dad even tried to help me get some clients as well, but it was a lot harder than I thought it was going to be. The Russian guy who owned the business was pushing his BS onto me saying how easy it was for him and I wasn't trying hard enough. Regardless, I found it impossible to get any revenue going. It was now the end of winter. I was getting stressed with my money running out. As I got more frustrated with the realisation, I had made a bad decision to leave the sinking corporate ship, slowly things started getting faster, in my mind that is. It was the beginning of spring, and I didn't know it, but I was manic again.

CHAPTER 23
The Floods Of Noah

After a few months and zero success with trying to sell the callback service, I began putting myself under pressure, mainly due to the fact I was not making sales and I left a reasonable and regular paycheck for a BS dream job with no pay. The cold of winter was gone, and spring had arrived. The days were warm, but the nights were still cool. If I could look at a bipolar weather map, I would be able to see the manic front approaching but I had no bipolar radar then and I had a year without any elevations. Sure, I may have been a tad on the low side, but I managed to be able to face the world.

As for my mate DC and the other peeps at PacStar? Well, most of them stuck around a few extra months and they did just fine. The wheels finally fell off that division of Telecom NZ and three months after I left everyone that stayed got a handsome payout of about twenty thousand dollars each. I felt like a real goose. Me and my stupid idea to cut and run. Sure, I was hanging to be working for myself again, but three extra months pay and a severance to sit back on would have given me time to relax and find a really good job, rather than the rubbish one I decided to take up.

I didn't realise, but the eye of the manic storm was getting closer and closer. I had lasted through a year with no hospital interventions, and I began to go through a denial phase about my bipolar diagnosis. I was smoking a lot of weed. I thought it was going to help as I could not sleep. This really became a huge issue for me. I feared going to sleep, thinking that if I did go to sleep, I was not going to wake up. Crazy right? Well, not everyone wakes from their sleep. But this was my mind playing games on me.

I would be up for two or more nights at a time, only sleeping when I could no longer stay awake. My sleep debt increased and so did my manic behaviour. Yep, I was in full denial which also meant that I didn't believe I had to take my meds. I was flying into a storm with zero visibility and no instruments. The only thing I had was pot and I was smoking an ounce a week to try and bring some relief from the agitation of the mania.

Smoking that much pot may not be a lot by Rastafarian standards, but to most pot smokers, it is a fair amount. The mania was running hard through my veins and my mind was beginning to play games with me again. I was borderline psychotic. While pot can have a calming effect and help, at this stage of my mania it was like throwing bricks down the Grand Canyon. I was stoned with racing thoughts and the agitation was off the hook. I was really strung out.

The one thing that I enjoyed at around 3 am each morning was a relaxing bath. I had a bit of a routine with this in these early morning hours. I found the water did help calm me down so on this one early spring morning I went to the bathroom to get the water going. We lived in an art deco building, built circa 1940. I think the bathtub was still the original huge cast iron tub which I really enjoyed. I got the water temperature right between the separate hot and cold taps and rather than stand there and wait for the tub to fill up I went into my study and sat down at my computer.

I got into whatever I was doing on the computer and was totally distracted. Suddenly, my ears picked up the sound of water hitting the ground outside. My flat was on the first floor so the sound of the water hitting the ground was quite noticeable. I looked outside the window to see if it was raining and noticed that it wasn't. I remember thinking to myself, it's not raining tonight how odd, where is the water coming from? I looked out and it was pouring from the side of the building, and then the penny dropped.

THE BATH!

I ran from my study past the lounge room to see the water already flooding halfway down the hallway. I entered the flooded bathroom and turned the taps off. Luckily there was a small hole between the bathroom and the outside wall which was there for this kind of accident. It wasn't a big hole but that was where the water was escaping through before splashing onto the ground. In the bathroom, the water was at least an inch high, and it flooded halfway down the entrance hallway of the flat and the carpet was not just soaked, it was a swamp.

Well, instead of having a relaxing bath, I was mopping up the carpet for hours. I was lucky not to drown all the cockroaches, the added thought of insect genocide could have added to my stressful situation. I was totally freaked out by what had happened, and by the time I finished mopping up the mess it was around 6 am. I was ready to pour another bath now but this time I sat in the bathroom and waited for the bathtub to fill up.

My mind was still running fast, but my body was exhausted. I settled into the bath. I was so freaked out by what had happened, my mind just could not relax. While I was not having any audible hallucinations like I did with my first mania, I was having some crazy thoughts about how I left a good paying job to start a commission-only position and yes, I became the whipping master. I was now under financial pressure while my colleagues were patient and well rewarded for it. The thought of my new job not working out was driving me insane, and I was driving myself insane. Not that I realised it, but now looking back I was clearly manic.

In the few months prior, I had also started to study numerology. What I really should be telling you is that it was not so much the study of numerology. Well, it started out that way, but it became an obsession of numerology. I would add numbers up, in all sorts of situations, and these numbers would have meanings to me. I could take a deck of cards and learnt various patterns with the cards, and I would interpret those as well. If I went to the gas station to fill up my car, I would look at the price on the gas pump add it up then round it down to a single digit and that meant something to me. Don't ask me now because I have forgotten but it was an obsession for sure.

These were not words from G-d as I really tried to keep it real regarding what I chose to believe, but my thinking was not right. The morning rolled on and I had done the best I could with the wet carpet. It was about 10 am and suddenly, I felt I needed some sort of spiritual energy around me. I just needed to feel some positive spiritual reinforcement to reassure me that things were okay. I drove to the synagogue on Flood Street that had now become a great place of learning for me. It then dawned on me that this synagogue happens to be on Flood Street. Now that didn't bother me too much, it was more of a thought, I had a flood in my flat and now I am in the synagogue on Flood Street, funny coincidence.

As I sat in one of the pews waiting for the Rabbi to come out and wrap the *tefillin* on me, I happened to pick up the weekly newspaper which always had a two-page breakdown of the weekly Torah *parsha* (portion). As I started to read on, I could not believe my eyes, as there just happened to be an explanation of this week's *parsha* which was about the story of Noah and the great flood. I could not believe it. Now this was just too much of a coincidence for me to cope with, my brain went into meltdown. As Jews we do not believe in coincidence, so these combined facts led me to believe it was now some kind of message I was receiving. First the flood at my place, then seeing this weekly scripture about Noah, surely there had to be some hidden message there.

I slowly became unhinged, and I lost it. I was asking one of the young *bocherim* (rabbinical students) to ask the Rabbi to come out as fast as possible as I needed him to put the boxes on me immediately! I needed to be closer to G-d because there were some evil thoughts just playing with my mind and I was losing it. Remember I had not had any sleep, so I was going out of my mind. The Rabbi came out, and he helped me with the *tefillin*, and I was somewhat relieved. They could see I was not in a good way, and they suggested I go see this Rabbi at Jewish House, which was on the same street, just down the road.

I spoke to the Rabbi at Jewish House, and he must have thought to himself that I was just not right in my thinking. I was manic, talking at a million miles an hour and all over the place. He asked me to take a seat, but I just bolted home. I went back to my place scribbled some of my numerology onto a page, and I drove back to Jewish House to show this Rabbi some of my numerology. Well, I don't think he needed anymore convincing than that, and now he was 100-percent sure that I was out of my mind, out of control and this was beyond anything that he could deal with.

So, he asked me to take a seat, I had no idea why. I sat there patiently not knowing where he went. Little did I know he went off to call in the cavalry. Fifteen minutes later, four police entered the building and said, 'Peter, you're going to have to come with us.' Naturally I didn't want to go fearing I was going to cop another month in the cooler. But common sense somehow kicked in and they were armed with all the right toys so there was no point in making a fuss. I was so pissed off. I could not believe I was being hauled away again in the back of a paddy wagon to my home away from home for an evaluation.

I didn't argue and complied with the officers, and as the paddy wagon pulled up and then entered through the gate of the laughing academy, the big steel gate closed shut behind me and I had a terrible sinking feeling that I was indeed in for another fully paid vacation, in the house of broken dreams, The Kiloh Centre, Prince of Wales Hospital. I was looking at another month at least.

CHAPTER 24
Mania Number Two: Back In The Cooler

The paddy wagon drove up onto a circular metal plate which spun the wagon in the right direction for them to leave, with the gate still shut. The van may have been facing the right direction, but there was no way I was going to be in it when they left.

Before I went inside to the waiting room, I had a horrible feeling that I was indeed in for another fully paid vacation in the house of broken dreams. The Kiloh Centre, Prince of Wales Hospital, AKA the puzzle factory, nut farm, laughing academy, call it what you will. I was looking at another month at least.

I sat in the waiting room on the wrong side of the locked doors and finally some doctors came out to evaluate me. It took them a fair while to come out, but when they did, I have to say they came to their conclusion pretty fast. The ruling came down against me and I was now officially booked in for who knows how long, once more. Had I known, I could have at least packed some fresh undies, socks, chocolate, and some suntan lotion. Okay, maybe I didn't need the suntan lotion, I was already fried.

This was going to be round three, and by now I was no freshman, so I knew what to expect. Did it make it any easier? No, not at all. It's like someone pushing a pause button on your life and you are back in the hands of others, with a fine assortment of roommates and their unique personalities to work out. I would have preferred to just wind this mania down at home, but there was no option for that. Had I realised myself I was indeed manic, I might have had half a chance, but that option was now well and truly gone. I was back in the house of *"do not argue"*, and *"obey all the rules, or else"*.

One look at my file and the doctors would have had enough history for them to make a snap call as to what to do with me. I'm sure they would have said, 'We better keep this one under close observation.'

Boy was I so pissed off! I mean come on! I was definitely going to miss my appointment at the nail salon tomorrow. While I didn't have a psychotic episode in the traditional sense, I was undoubtedly manic. If only I had been aware then that trying to survive on minimal sleep for weeks would be enough to make me manic, I might have been able to turn things around.

Avoiding sleep would drive anyone insane, no matter If you had bipolar or not. Back then I didn't realise it was so important. All the other stuff that occurred on the morning of my arrest such as the flood in my flat, reading about the great flood in the weekly scripture – well that was not coincidence, but I let it get the better of me. Being that elevated, who knows what might have happened to me, and I hate to say this, but it was probably the best place for me to be at the time.

I was wound up and needed to have that pressure released in a controlled and monitored environment. That place may be called a hospital but to me it is still a prison for the mentally unwell. I was angry about getting hauled in there, but I certainly didn't argue with my doctors as I knew I had to avoid the *"don't argue"* dart of slumber. No way I wanted to cop that again. That stuff will put you into earth's orbit for a good two days. No thanks. Deep inside I was the ultimate angry insect but nonetheless had to cop it sweet, as they say.

Back in the laughing academy. Nothing like a month in the cooler to bring me back to reality. It was confusing again, as I really wanted to believe that I didn't have bipolar, but this was another confirmation that indeed I had the condition. I was only deceiving myself thinking that I didn't need to take my condition seriously.

It was heartbreaking. It was back to the regime of super dosing my meds along with the crappy hospital food once more, not to mention the vampires taking blood every day. It was a bitch. Then of course there were my fellow inmates who are in their own world of pain, which, as usual, was hard to watch. Dealing with some of these people gave me the shits. I am sure I gave them the shits as well. Everyone seemed to be on edge, and it was hard to watch their behaviour, not all of them, but in the acute ward there were mainly people like me. They were coming down from their own mental anguish, psychosis, or mania. Sometimes it was irritating, at other times slightly amusing. They all had their own stories of how they ended up here. I would befriend one or two. Sometimes their stories were amusing, at other times hard to listen to.

Now I should be grateful for the bed and three meals, breakfast was fine, but the lunch and dinners were always some kind of meat and veggies which were always more steamed than my brain. The chef was definitely not Chinese.

The days of boring TV or DVD's and pacing around the locked ward rolled by. I could usually find one person I could talk to, and those conversations were interesting. Especially with the schizophrenics, they had some of the most interesting tales. But we were all in there being treated to get out as fast as the doctors could bring us back to earth. I could not help but think of some people who may have taken too much acid and just not come back. That is tragic.

As before, I started off in the acute ward. There were 10 rooms with nine other men on my side of the acute ward. Adjacent was the women's acute ward with 10 rooms for them. Did I mention that the acute wards were a very confined space and can be quite dangerous? There are no fines nor charges of assault in a psych ward. Should there be a disagreement between men or women, it's sorted out on a one-on-one basis, sometimes with a good punch to the head.

If the alarms went off, because one of the cellmates just went nuts, then it was going to be a spectacular show of strength. Mainly from the staff of orderlies who would come running in from all directions to calm the incident down. And boy did they come in numbers when the shit hit the fan. When the alarm went off, I would also run to see what the fuss was about. It may have been one person, or two. If the situation called for the riot squad, both people involved, or the individual would be dragged off to cop the needle.

The air in those wards was always filled with tension and frustration, with a side of confusion. Nobody wants to be locked up against their will. There is also a lot of bewilderment as to why we have ended up in this situation. I suppose that is why we get the time to cool our heads. It's time for reflection without the koi fishpond. One minute we are free, then the next we are dragged away from society, mostly in a manic or psychotic headspace. Locked up by law under the *Mental Health Act 2015* (the Act), until the doctors medicate us enough to parachute us gently back to earth with a soft landing.

Staying calm in the confines of those wards is not easy either. The acute ward doesn't have much space, so it is not easy to avoid people. The outside courtyard didn't offer much solace either. It was a confined space with way too many hotheads wandering around. Escape as usual was impossible, but not far from some people's minds.

Thankfully after two very long and boring weeks, I was rewarded for my good behaviour, and I was moved to the general ward. It was a relief to be in a bigger space, with more people in the general ward, I now knew I was not far off from being granted lunchtime leave. In the general ward, it is mixed, so men and women can wander freely. Two days later, I was asked to see the head nurse who gave me the good news that I was allowed to go out at lunchtime for one hour starting from tomorrow. This was something I looked forward to. It wasn't much time but at least I could see life beyond the locked doors and walls of the general ward.

The next day I could hardly wait to go out to the nearby shopping centre, where I bought my lunch and some food items to snack on later. Walking back to the hospital and finally being buzzed back into the general ward was hard as I didn't really want to go back in. I had no choice. If I didn't return then they would have the police look for me and once caught, I would be back into the acute ward, with my time starting all over again.

I had my wits about me and enough common sense to understand that the brief lunch break was also a test to make sure I was being compliant. For a fleeting moment I thought about doing a runner. It was only a brief thought, as I knew it was only about two more weeks and I would be a free man. Time rolled by with the same mundane ways to amuse myself, mostly thinking about how it all unravelled this time.

I could not help but look back and reflect on how this mania seemed to just sneak up on me and fill my brain and body with so much energy, which I tried to calm down with my own self medicating. I didn't realise I was elevated, and I completely failed to reel in that manic energy. I think if someone told me that my behaviour was off during this second mania, I doubt I would have believed them. Had they said to me that I should go and get checked out by my psych doctor, I probably would have told them that they were the crazy one and perhaps they should be going to see a shrink. That was pure denial. After the first mania I was always checking the thoughts in my mind.

I was not hearing voices or having some kind of prophetic thoughts in my head, so I would think that I was fine, but looking back now with a non-elevated mind I could see that indeed my motor was running hot.

These signs were:

1. The changing of seasons from winter to spring

2. Lack of, and fear of sleep

3. Self-medicating with way too much weed

4. Becoming totally obsessed with numerology, letting the numbers rule my life.

5. Making a bad career decision.

6. Not taking my prescribed medicines to deal with my mania.

Not thinking the career move through properly was an added pressure I just didn't need. It really was the flame that got my mania going. I had put myself under pressure again just like I had during my first mania. I left my mundane but well-paid job for a commission-only gig. There wasn't even an advance against future commission, I was sold a pipe dream. This business was good for some who had entered early in the game. I knew some people who did this and made good money with it, but for me it was nothing more than steam. I found it hard getting clients to use the callback service. I should have been patient and stayed with my job at the telco until I found a good job with a base salary. Instead, this bad decision left me with minimal savings, and a head full of worry.

I started this new job and put crazy pressure on myself to do it well. I also had unrealistic expectations as to how easy it was going to be. Yeah, this was the gasoline that really got my mind going and looking back, it hurt. The pain of not getting any traction also made me question my skills as a salesperson. Maybe that was a bit of self-doubt from the black cloud that was creeping in.

Nobody wants to admit to making a bad career move. Money, that's just a by-product from the work and effort we put into our career. For me I really have to love or at least like and believe in what I do. This last gig was a real grind. If you put in the effort, you deserve the reward. However, this job was a real fizzler. It was hard not to look back on everything that happened over the past year. The first mania, then suicidal depression which was so hard to come back from. But I did though.

Getting the job at the telco was a positive, but then I didn't need another move in the wrong direction. I had already lost my credibility, my business, any material wealth I had including that darn watch, and worst of all, my Sydney privileges. I lost people who I thought were my friends (these days they are just people I know). But they are not. They stay well away due to my new label, either frightened of me or my behaviour. Who knows, they may think that bipolar is contagious.

I think that is the worst part, being stigmatised with this condition. Without a doubt it is one of the worst things. Nobody wants to be labelled unless it's with a positive tag. Those labels came from people who wanted to be judge, and social executioner. It hurt on one level. On another, it didn't matter at all. I knew I was bigger than that. But when you're in a negative headspace, it takes a lot to put all that has happened behind and rebuild. I had to dig deep to find where that other level of me was, and I knew it was not in the physical world. It was in the spiritual world. I had started or maybe I was forced into a journey that was my destiny. Who knows, it could have been that or something worse.

I didn't understand the spiritual, as I had zero Jewish education. So, it was going to be baby steps. But for me, I knew they were steps in the right direction. When you have nothing, sometimes faith is all you need. Of course, there were a lot of questions that needed answering and it was during this time in the general ward that gave me time to question so many things. But it was also another time to accept things about myself including my condition which whipped me right back to the dorms of the insane and deeply depressed.

I was working out where I was between those two choices, and I preferred to not be insane, although I did manage to work myself up into a state again that's for sure. I could ask myself, why? Why make a bad career move? Why put all that pressure on myself? The answer was simple. I just wanted to be working for myself again. It was all I ever wanted after leaving the music industry. It was the dream Version 2.0. I got there and I had my own business for five years, then I lost the business, lost my mind, had one go at ending it all, then the slow crawl back to happy land had begun again.

I managed to get a good paying job. Had I not been able to get that job, I could have ended up unemployed for a long time. I had spent long enough being the whipping master over what went down. I was ready to move on. I had to push myself and build up my confidence to be able to get that job at Telecom NZ. I should have had the patience to just stick it out a bit longer.

Doing a crap corporate gig sucks. Having to put on a suit and tie and sell something that you find boring is not fun. It was a means to an end, but it was a gig that was good for my confidence, and I had also made a good friend. It sure beat the hell out of staying home and doing nothing. I reached that point where I was mentally strong enough to do that job. I was doing fine in that job as well. I knew that things were heading south for the company because there were other people, mainly senior managers that had their parachutes packed and they were jumping ship. I got itchy feet as well. I have no idea why I put the pressure on myself, but I did. Working for Telecom NZ was an education and insight into how a big telco operates. It was certainly an eye-opener.

Living in Sydney had its own pressures. It is a competitive city with lots to offer. Leaving TCNZ was a mistake. I got sold a pipe dream with the new job and I made a bad career move. So, I made a mistake with my career. Big deal. It's easy to say that now with hindsight. That wasn't the only problem. I was doing all this analysis while I was still locked in the general ward. I had to look back. Not too far, just far enough to do enough of a post-mortem so I didn't make the same mistakes again.

I had no real plan. I was probably about to slide into a depression. After all, what goes up in the bipolar world does come crashing down. This was the first time that the police were called out to take me away. It was not pleasant. I went along quietly, with no pushback so that was one good thing. I mean they were there to do their job and I had enough common sense to not give any pushback.

Looking back on what happened has to be the ultimate torture. It is also not productive. It is okay to do some retrospection, if not how else can we learn from our mistakes? Being stuck in those locked wards with not much to do, I had way too much spare time to think, and I could not help but think of how this mania deceived me and spun my brain into overdrive.

I had to look back to try and understand how the mania got the better of me. I had to learn the hard way because I took things into my own hands and didn't manage it properly as per my doctor's instructions. Worst of all, I had to accept the truth, and there was no way I could be in denial, that indeed I had bipolar type 1. That was the hardest thing to accept, again.

I was doing well working and holding down a job. My thinking during that period was fine. I had no mania. There was no psychosis, and I thought I was for the better part, grounded. I would like to say again that not everyone with bipolar type 1 is going to have the same things trigger them. Yes, it was that combination of things that I mentioned earlier that set me off. The mania just snuck in and twisted my thinking to make me believe what it wanted me to believe.

It was good to identify where my thinking went wrong and how I got carried away with this second mania. For now, I had to get the F out of the puzzle factory and start the rebuild, yet again. I questioned myself, wondering if I will ever have my own business again. I had no idea as to how I could do that. The doctors in this place were doing a good job in bringing me down from my mania, and the slide into depression had begun. I just had to prove to myself that I was indeed sane.

While I did get manic, looking forward I felt I still had what it takes to be able to one day be in business for myself again. With no ideas or funds, I knew I had to start all over again by getting another job. The thought of that was daunting, I knew I had a negative head at that moment, and that was overwhelming. I thought about the man who managed to talk me into the crap job I had been doing. To be honest, he was not such a bad person, but he did talk it up big and how easy it was to win business. Leaving my well-paid job for a position I really didn't evaluate properly was well, stupid, or gullible and all my fault.

If only I looked at my behaviour closely and joined the dots, I might have avoided this trip to the puzzle factory. Today, it would be so clear to me as I am more aware, but back then, it wasn't. This was my second mania, and I was still doing my apprenticeship in bipolarism. It is easy to look back with hindsight, we become the smartest person in the room. Had the Rabbi from Jewish House not called the cops, the mania would have just rolled on and on and who knows what other damage I would have done. So, I have to thank him for looking out for me. He really did the right thing. Even though at the time I was super pissed off.

The days and weeks rolled by, and I had been a model patient at the laughing academy. Eventually my time had come, and I was put before a panel of doctors and nurses about seven or eight people. It was a lot. It was like a scene out of *12 Monkeys*. They asked me a whole series of questions for about 40 minutes to evaluate my headspace, and then I was allowed to go back to my room.

It was a sanity check for sure. Was I really sane and ready to pass their test? Of course I was. I had come back down from my elevation and fast brain rotations. Whatever they put in the ice cream and late-night Milo worked. Nothing cools you down like a stint in that place. It is a real leveller. Once they get you in that place, you will be forced under strict supervision, to come back to earth via every trick in the book they have. So, if you should sadly end up at the laughing academy, do not resist, their intentions only mean well. If you don't comply, then they will put you down to sleep your bad attitude off, and boy are their drugs strong. I'm sure they could keep you in suspended animation for as long as it is required. They have brute force as well so please take my advice and don't muck them around.

By the way, about those hard-core drugs, don't get too excited as they are not recreational. They are medicinal brain lock drugs. Once they inject you with that stuff, you go down faster than a Mike Tyson punch to the head. Yes, I have to say it is best to avoid that place if possible. They are a bit like a casino. The house wins every time. Try beating the house. Well good luck with that. My only advice is to be on your best behaviour. They will let you go when they know you're ready to leave. For me it was all about to be put in the past. I was about to get the best news I'd had in weeks.

I think the day was a Friday, and I was told that on Monday I was being released to go home. Fantastic! This was the best news I'd had in a long time. The 48-hour wait was going to seem like six months, but at least there was a green light ahead of me and I had something to look forward to. I thought of what it might be like to be in another type of prison. In 1989, I managed to escape that, luckily. Did I have a get out of jail free card? Not as far as I could tell. I had a great contact who helped me find a great barrister. I could have got six months to five years for that, but I was lucky to avoid that trip. But that's another story…

Me and my parents c1982.

Seraphine Radnai, my grandmother.

Dad loved all animals, his camera at here the ready, for a photo opportunity.

My Mother also loved animals, she is with our dog Lucy.

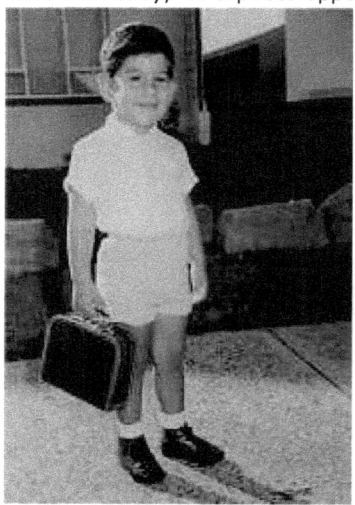

Heading off to my first 'business meeting' at kindergarten, aged 5.

This guitar was just a toy, but to me it was serious Rock & Roll, aged 7.

BIPOLAR HEAD

 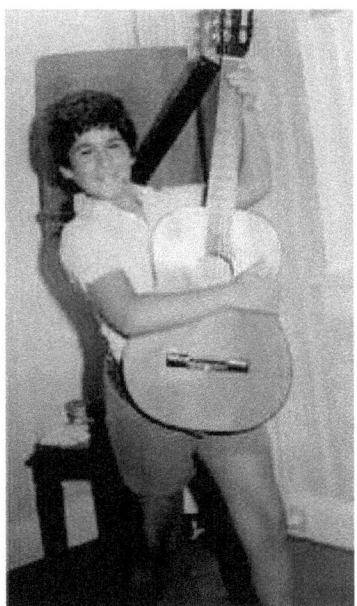

I was blessed with a happy childhood. My happy place.

Here I am with my new Brad Haynes .   Gardening in between gigs.
custom surfboard, aged 15

At 15, I was totally obsessed with two things: surfing and *Kiss*.

The T-shirt says it all, aged 17.

Publicity photoshoot, taken by my dad in his Parisian Studios, aged 20, 1984

Playing at a private function c1988.   Banged up abroad, 2014.

Video still performing *Body Talk*, with the band *Koo Dé Tah*

Playing a gig with Sticky Fingers for the Finks Motorcycle Club, Coffs Harbour in the '90s.

The Resort's resident band, The Covers: LtoR: Tony Leon (piano/vocals), Steve Promphrett (bass), Dale Nougher (keyboards), Peter Radnai (electronic drums/percussion) and Ken Davis (LinnDrum/guitar/keyboards).

Koo Dé Tah: LtoR: John Bettison, Tina Cross, Peter Radnai, Capree Morris, Roger Faynes, Leon Berger.

Rambatan's mountain-top view overlooking World Heritage-listed Dorrigo National Park, Northern Tablelands, New South Wales, Australia.

The Thunderbox at *Rambatan* had big view, and never backed up!

Rambatan, the house looked like it the was straight out of a fairytale.

CHAPTER 25
1989, That Other Story

As mentioned, the year was 1989. I was living in a Victorian terrace house with a dear friend of mine, Shimon. Both of us had not discovered religion at this stage of our lives and I suppose the best way to describe us was that we were a pair of naughty Jewish lads who loved to get high.

Shimon had left his country of birth, South Africa and migrated to Australia with his family in the late '70s. It was the first wave of the South African migration to arrive in Sydney's Jewish community. For me and my friends, these new immigrants were exotic aliens who were smart, sassy and they talked with a familiar, yet strange tone of English that to my ears was at first something quite intriguing. It was exciting for us as we now had more Jewish friends, but the stories that they told from their homeland seemed quite frightening to me. I could not imagine living in a country with such social turmoil. These immigrants, like my parents, just wanted a better life in a country that had on the surface, equal opportunity for those that landed here.

They were different to my parents who came here with nothing; annihilation of family, persecution, and zero material wealth. They seemed to come with experience, and were able to move some of their money out even though it was limited. They emigrated to Australia as a complete family unlike my mother, who only had her brother. Her parents and sister and her sister's three-year-old son, all murdered in the camps of Auschwitz. Or my father who was an only child, his father murdered by the Hungarians when the Germans told them it was a free for all to murder or use Jews for slave labour. My father being younger and stronger, was rounded up in those slave labour camps. I could never imagine, (although I have tried on so many occasions) what it must have been like for my parents to witness these atrocities. It was not a day or a week, but months and ultimately a year of having to endure this horror.

These new immigrants assimilated into our community well. Their parents came with a wealth of business and professional skills, and we made friends with the new South African kids. They were smart, entertaining to be around and the girls just happened to be gorgeous as well. Their parents were also very welcoming in their homes, so many of us loved to hang out at their places. Some of the parents were quite liberal and tolerated us smoking weed in our friends' bedroom as well. I know this would not have gone down well at all in my house.

Prior to 1989 and before I was a professional musician, I had studied two years of horticulture at The Ryde School of Horticulture. While I had a genuine interest in all things that grew from an early age, I was particularly fond of growing pot. They say if you can grow tomatoes, then you can grow pot, but there was a bit more to it than that.

Certain leaves need to be pruned at the right time, the feeding formula needs to be balanced with the right food, the temperature needs to be correct for the vegetative growth and then lowered for the flower cycle. If you succeed with all of that, then you can pull your plants and begin the drying which cannot be rushed. It needs to be dried properly, in a well-ventilated room, and this can take about 10 to 12 days.

I had never grown an indoor crop under lights before and neither had Shimon. Both of us had grown a plant or two outside, but doing something indoors was a whole different matter. Well Shimon and I decided that we were going to give it a proper go, and we rented a terrace house in the inner Sydney suburb of Glebe. These semi-detached Victorian terraces had a minimum of two to three levels. Downstairs were the living rooms, kitchen, and bathroom, while upstairs were two bedrooms. From my bedroom there was a set of pull-down stairs which led into a big attic space. This was out of the way and a perfect space for our indoor gardening project. In hindsight I should have put some kind of covering across the ceiling so no one could see the rectangular cut out from where the stairs came down, but I wasn't really having people over, and it was not very obvious, so I didn't bother.

Once we had moved in, we set up the garden in the attic under lights. The idea at first was to start with a large number from the seeds that we had and then cull them down to the females that we wanted to keep. We didn't have an idea as to how many we were going to grow, and we started with about 150 or so. We didn't even count or have an idea as to how many we were going to end up with, we just took the seeds that we had and germinated them. We didn't think it through as we had not picked any particular strain. The science of indoor growing and availability of indoor strains was not yet widely available. These were random seeds we had collected over time.

As the seeds germinated, we then placed them into small plastic cups. The cups were filled with a growing medium of perlite and vermiculite, and we fed them with a hydroponic vegetative growth solution. The plants seemed to be quite happy, and it was the very start of the grow, they were tiny.

Being the naughty lads or drug fiends that we were, we could not pass up on the idea of having some cocaine sent to us from one of Shimon's contacts in Los Angeles. The price of cocaine has always been ten times more expensive here in Sydney, and our intentions were to sell some to cover our cost and have the rest to share. I wish we had some other hairbrained scheme, but we just couldn't help ourselves, so we sent the money overseas and arranged for an ounce of blow to be sent to us from Shimon's contact. Of course, we had the envelope addressed to an anonymous name, and then we waited.

I think we were so excited when finally, the wait was over, and the mailman delivered the letter. I got a call from Shimon; I was at work, and he told me the letter had arrived. I left work and headed home with excitement thinking we did it. When I got home, I looked at my front door with disbelief as it had been smashed in. There was a sledgehammer in the door frame and when I looked inside, there were men in suits walking around frantically. I stood there in shock, and one came up to me and asked, 'Who are you?'

I could not lie. I said, 'I live here.'

'Come in,' he said.

I walked inside past the first room and into the lounge room. There I saw Shimon standing with a towel around his waist, and soap still in his hair. He was looking at me with the biggest deer eyes a man could possibly have. Apparently, he was in the shower when the Australian Federal Police (AFP) knocked on the front door. Not hearing their knock, those cowboys just smashed the front door down, found Shimon in the shower and put a gun to his head and asked him to get out, really slowly. He'd obviously called me prior to taking the shower, and fortunately for us he didn't open the letter.

There were ten of them in total. We had been separated and two of the Feds asked me to come with them as they wanted to search my bedroom. I walked up the narrow stairs and they began their search of my room. One opened my bedside draw and found a half ounce of pot with a book on how to grow indoor hydroponics. He was throwing stuff all over the place lifting my mattress, searching under my bed, while the other officer was going through my clothes and wardrobe. They found a bag containing all my personal mail since I was a teen. That was confiscated, and I stood there watching in disbelief as my world was being thrown upside down.

This defiling of my room continued for about 40 minutes. It was like a scene in a movie when the cops just go through everything with no respect, throwing all my possessions and clothes on the floor. It was not only violating but humiliating at the same time. One of the officers then asked me if I had any plants. I said no. He said he was going to go down to the garden to check. I said, 'No problem, go and take a look down there.'

Just as he was walking out of my bedroom, he happened to look up at the ceiling and he noticed the rectangular cut out and he asked, 'What's up there?'

What's up there is none of your business, I thought to myself. 'Oh, it's just some storage space.'

He then asked if he could take a look. At this point I think my world went into slow motion as I didn't think it was going to matter what I said to him. He was going to have a look whether I liked it or not.

'Sure, take a look.'

At that point I just remember thinking to myself, now I am really going to be screwed. He grabbed the broom handle with the hook on the end of it used it to pull the stairs down and started to walk up the stairs. When he popped his head up into the attic, he called out to his fellow officer standing in my room saying, 'Hey Robbo, you better call the Sarge. It looks like Hawaii up here.'

From that moment, my heart sank as I knew that the letter downstairs was now no longer our biggest problem, our little garden project was just moved into the 'you are now totally screwed' category. If I could throw up, I would have. Shimon was in his room having his world thrown upside down, and I was not sure if he had any idea that the weed had been discovered. Well, if he didn't realise or hear the Feds call out for their Sergeant to take a look at what they had found, he certainly was going to find out soon enough.

From that moment on, it didn't really matter what happened next, my life was about to change, and I was about to experience my year from hell. Yes, the bipolar health issues I have written about so far were no picnic, and losing one's marbles and the slow crawl back to sanity was hard, but being enveloped in the legal system, having to face criminal charges, was sickening. I had no idea what was to come or how I was going to get out of it.

When the AFP had done what they needed to do and were convinced that there was nothing left for them to find in the house, we were both taken to police headquarters which at the time was in the TNT Towers in Redfern. I was so sick in my stomach I could hardly breathe. I thought for sure that this time I had pushed it way too far, and I am going to go to jail. Shimon and I had been kept apart and it was time for our statements to be taken. I was not sure what Shimon was going to say. Regarding the grow, they assumed that we had both done this and so we were both charged with the cultivation.

As for the half ounce of weed they found in my draw, and the other half ounce which was found in Shimon's room, and because I told them that I went to buy the pot, and we went halves, they actually charged me with supply, that was such a stitch-up and totally unfair. Yes, I went to grab it for us, but to be charged with selling Shimon the weed? Crazy. If only they had any idea how many times he had gone out to score us weed. I should have kept my mouth shut and told them that I had no idea how it got there. Of course, then they wanted to know who I got the weed from, and I told them I had bought it from someone whom I only recognised by their face, down at the pub. I was not going to rat on anyone.

The interrogation went on for hours. I think in total I was there for about eight hours. They asked me about the letter, and I said I had no idea about the letter. There was not much they could do to prove it was ours. Fortunately for us, Shimon didn't open the mail. Had he done so, we would have been up on a charge for that as well.

If only I had covered the ceiling in my bedroom, I would have saved us the most serious charge of all, which was cultivation of the plants. Unlike Shimon and I, the Feds did count all the seedlings and there were 180 of them in total. The law in the state of New South Wales states as follows: It doesn't matter how big or small your marijuana plant is, the fine is two thousand dollars per plant. If your plant weighs a pound or they are just a seedling, it doesn't matter, the fine is still two thousand dollars per plant. This being the case, they valued our crop at three hundred and sixty thousand dollars. Now that was a total joke. All in all, there would not have been more than five or six ounces of dried crap leaf there. How on earth could they value those little seedlings at such an astronomic amount of money?

After the interrogation by the Feds, I was so dejected, I didn't know what to do or where to go, so I headed over to my mother's place. She took one look at me and right away said, 'You're in trouble, aren't you?'

I said, 'Yes, big trouble.'

Then my mother who had survived the worst that life could throw at you said something that I will never forget. She said, 'No matter what it is, we will get through this.'

Just like that, I looked at my mother who survived Auschwitz, and suffered so much in life and I was totally blown away. I felt this comfort from her strength and all that she had been through and with those words I felt the strength of a woman who beat adversity and death on a daily basis. When she said those words, a feeling of relief came over me. She was not happy with me, but no matter what, she had my back and was in my corner for the fight. Together we were going to face what was to come and beat it.

It gave me a whole new perspective of my mother. She had always been one who dished out the tough love, and while I was expecting her to rip shreds off me, she was my greatest support in my hardest battle. Going to court is no joke. Being charged and then the thought of the unknown with potentially a custodial sentence to beat is extremely serious. It is the fight of your life. Let's face it, nobody wants to go to jail.

It is like you're in a raft on a wild river with no paddle to help you, and you're totally at the mercy of the river. Getting the best person to represent you is key to winning. But I knew nobody in this profession. I had a neighbour who had beaten some charges a while back and I gave him a call, telling him that I was in trouble. He asked me to come to his office and I met with him there the next day. I explained the circumstances and he told me not to worry, he knew the best barrister for me.

This was a great relief. I rang the barrister the next day and made an appointment to see him. We discussed the matter, and he told me that he could not guarantee that I would get off, but there was a very good chance that I could. Shimon went to his own barrister who said he is looking at six months minimum to five years jail time. Needless to say, he switched over to my guy.

The next nine months were going to teach me what it was like to be entangled in the legal system. To start with, there were two of the Feds who were on my tail harassing me at work, coming there during business hours. Naturally, I took them outside to answer any questions that they had. They were really trying to pin the letter on me, asking me questions and hoping that I would crack and give in with some kind of admission. But I refused.

We had to move out of the house and quickly find alternative living arrangements. I could not relax. My waking hours were filled with worry and the possibility of doing some time in the big house. Months rolled by, and I managed to keep my job.

Finally, the day arrived when we went to court. The matter was heard in the district court, which is not the court of petty sessions, this court was for more serious offences. I just remember my barrister telling me to bring a toothbrush with me! He had a good sense of humour, but there was some truth in that we were possibly looking at some jail time.

As we waited outside, I remember my barrister coming up to us and he said, 'Guys I have some good news. We have been switched to another courtroom and judge.'

The judge we were first assigned to was apparently a bit of a "hanging judge", and the matter was now going to be heard in front of a more lenient judge. We entered the courtroom, and I could tell that the prosecutor was not organised at all. He seemed to be fumbling through his paperwork. I felt as if I was going to blackout, I was sick to my stomach. The prosecutor started and mentioned that there were 180 plants and that the value of this crop was three hundred and sixty thousand dollars. The judge who had pictures in front of him of the dried leaf matter then questioned the prosecutor saying, that this amount in the photo could not possibly be worth that much money. It would not even have been a pound of dried garbage leaf.

While he did recognise the law, he was also being realistic, and my barrister agreed, and stated the fact that we were just growing this for ourselves, and the amount could not possibly be worth anywhere near that ridiculous amount of money. The judge then asked the prosecutor and my barrister into his chambers. It was time for them to go behind the show of the courtroom and into his chambers to discuss how this was to play out.

On returning, the judge had considered the fact that this was our first offence and we had good references. He saw the deep regret and that we were truly remorseful for our actions. Right then and there I would have laid myself at his feet and begged him for leniency if that was possible, but of course this type of behaviour is just not on. As we both pleaded guilty to the cultivation, and possession of the weed found in our draw, the judge came down with his sentence.

By now, I was close to passing out. The courtroom was spinning around me as I was terrified of a custodial sentence. The sentence the judge handed down was an eight thousand dollar fine for each of us, along with a three-year good behaviour period. When we heard this, we could not believe it. We narrowly escaped a 'go to jail' card, and while the fine was hefty, we didn't have to do any community service, and we also got a 'no conviction' recorded. We could not have hoped for a better outcome. NO JAIL!

We thanked our barrister, saying what a genius he was. He just told us that we were lucky that at the last minute we had been changed over to a more lenient judge who was more realistic about what we had been caught with. That, along with whatever else he told the judge out the back in chambers worked in our favour. Having a prosecutor who got the brief five minutes before he walked in also helped. I could not imagine how my life would have changed had I been sent to the big house. Being locked up in there would have been horrific and changed me for sure. Apart from that, it is also such a stigma to be branded with that label as well as the one that I was going to get a few years later. G-d was shining down on us that day in court and gave us a massive blessing. For that I am forever grateful.

It was not over though. Remember how they charged me for supply of the half ounce of weed I scored for Shimon and myself? Well, I went to the lower court for that, and this time the prosecutor was gunning for me. I got another fine and more time added to my good behaviour period. Apparently now I had to behave for five years, and should I end up being presented in front of a court for so much as a joint in my possession, the whole events of these matters would be tried again, and I could end up in some serious trouble.

With that ended a period I never wish to go through again. Working out my mental health has been one battle against myself. There is no crime or anything illegal there. But having been locked up as I was for the short periods of time until I got better were what I called my time in jail for the mentally unwell.

No one wants to go there. I know I certainly didn't. But I had to go to cool my mind and return to earth because my bipolar mania just got out of hand. Lucky for me there is no crime in that. Although I am sure I have some lengthy records that one day I would like to read, when I am up for it. For now, life is good as I write this, but let's go back to the story.

I had just been hospitalised and brought back to reality. Of course, back then I was not feeling good like I am today. I was on the come down of being locked in there and about to come out with a head full of depression. It is just what happens when the staff of the puzzle factory bring you back to earth. I had been here before, so I knew what to expect. Did it make it easier? Not really. But I knew in time I was going to pick myself up. I was not there just yet. I was still in a world of pain.

CHAPTER 26
Back Home 1996 – The Post Mortem

Now that I had been released with the mania medicated out of me, the clouds of depression set in thick and fast. Looking back, it was like that movie *A Beautiful Mind*. If you haven't seen the movie, it is the true story about a brilliant mathematician and his struggle with schizophrenia. After a psychotic episode, to his disbelief, he found himself in the psych ward. When he was released, he struggled to accept his diagnosis. He was fine for a while, but then he went off his meds. So, in his unwell mind he thinks he is working for the government on some secret project, when really it was another psychotic episode.

All I have to say is, there were similarities for me. Just like the mathematician, I also got stung by my own mind during my first psychotic mania. The psychotic voice was so real I was terrified. After that I was doing well for almost a year. I also struggled like the mathematician to believe that I had this new label. I found it hard to accept. But one thing was for sure, after my first mania, I was going to question any voices I heard again. I wasn't going to believe just anything that came into my mind and take what I thought as the truth. I had to question everything.

I had decided after that first mania that the thoughts in my mind had to come from one of two sources. They were either coming from a positive or good source or they were coming from a negative and bad source. I held back on using the word 'evil' because while it exists, it just sounds too dramatic.

Being in denial was a huge problem for me, I believed all was well, and things were well for a while. But then the pressure of that new job, sleep deprivation, and then the self-medicating to help me with that horrific agitation, well that was clearly not doing the job. I thought the pot was what I needed to wind down, but it didn't work. It obviously didn't take the edge off and help me relax or get to sleep which was why I was smoking it in the first place. I needed proper meds to treat my mania and calm down that agitation. That feeling was horrible. I can only describe it like being a kettle that is boiling away, without being turned off. It is not pleasant. In hindsight, this clearly set me up for mania number two.

It made me sick to look back and run the replays of what had happened, but I could not help but do the post-mortem. Sadly, the playbacks are quite vivid, and I do remember them. Sometimes I wish I could choose to forget because my behaviour was just outrageous, atrocious, embarrassing, and downright not acceptable. Yes, I was unwell, and I can say that I was not in my right mind, but that excuse can only go so far.

Sure, over the years I have forgotten some stuff, but let's be clear that the behaviour when manic is like an alter ego, especially if I have turned green and into the hulk. But coming back from a recent mania, I do recall what went down. For some reason looking back is important as well because I try to work out exactly where the wheels fell off. That is not easy.

You would think that I would have gone through all of this in my mind in the hospital. Sure, I went through a lot of it. But let's not forget that my beauty treatment in the hospital went beyond my hair and nails being done. There was a lot of internal brain dampening with heavy doses of meds to bring me down from the manic high. I think that they had me doped up a fair amount for the first two weeks, and then as they started to back off the hard-core meds, I ran the plays in my mind.

How could I let the numerology get so out of control? I have to say I was loving it, but letting it take over my life? That's crazy. Oh, and by the way, don't think your life is not run by numbers. I can assure you today you will be using at least a few numbers between one and ten. Who knows you may even venture out into the top 20, or more. You may go and buy some items which add up to $67.50c, when adding these numbers together they total '18.' If you're Jewish '18' is a significant number, because the word *chai* which means 'life' which adds up to the number '18.' Each letter in Judaism corresponds to a number.

Relax, you will be fine. I am fine, I just got carried away with the numbers again for a moment. As you can see, I am still fond of the numbers, but now I treat it with respect and don't get carried away with it anymore. I don't allow them to rule my life the way it did during the mania.

Back during mania II, I obviously loved it too much. It became my obsession during this mania, and I was also just beginning my path into Judaism. I was starting from the right source, this time around, learning about *chassidus* which was totally new to me. I also went back to the Yeshiva to put on *tefillin* daily. I was so financially strapped I could not buy my own pair yet, but I now saw this as my daily spiritual medication, so I went to visit the Rabbi daily to have him help me with the *tefillin*.

The Rabbi told me not to get carried away, 'You have a day off once a week.'

'Really?' I asked.

He said, 'Yes, take Shabbat off, no *tefillin*. Okay?'

I had zero knowledge and I think it was overwhelming. At least
I was on the right path. It did spin me out though. They say a little knowledge
can be a dangerous thing, and with my new learning of my Jewish background
there was so much to take in. At least now at home I was also getting into being
spiritual from the right source. What do I mean by that? Well during mania
number one, I heard voices. Voices that wanted me to believe I was a prophet,
or the Messiah. This was a psychotic episode, no doubt about it. I can assure
you that I was none of the things that my mind tried to make me believe. It was
the psychosis that had led me to believe those things and it can be a very
powerful and deceptive voice in one's head. At the time I was under a lot of
pressure again, smoking weed to help with the agitation, and I think I just pushed
my mind to the point where I had cracked. The voices were audible
hallucinations, and it had me scared out of my mind.

While I found it hard to accept, the voices had me believe that what they were
saying was the truth. I didn't accept or believe it was indeed a psychotic episode.
Not until I went through the two rounds at the laughing academy. I feel that I
had trained my mind now to question what I heard in my head. I'm not going
believe just anything in my head anymore, and I have to question everything. If
I hear rubbish or think rubbish, I need to take that out with the mental garbage
right away. I need to know what I am thinking is real, not some fairytale or some
kind of fantasy. I need to know that the voice in my head is honest and coming
from a good source.

I messed up here again with this second mania and yes, I got sent off the field,
again, for another round at the laughing academy to take some serious
medication and a bloody long walk down the hall of mirrors to take a good look
at myself. Looking back this time I know where I went wrong. My bipolar radar
map was showing all clear skies, but that thing was jammed up so bad I had all
the wrong information, and I flew off course and paid the price with another
time out. Now I was stuck on the other side. I was out with not much to do, a
head full of depression, which was now becoming a standard in my life.

It was my BP depression V2.0.

Once again, I was in the dark fog, so depressed I could hardly get out of bed. I had no idea of how to get out from the black cloud. I knew that over time it does get better, and I had time. I had nothing else but time. I could not bear to wake in the mornings to see another day through with this depression.

'Hang in there', I tried to say to myself, but really, I felt as if my life was over.

The funk was horrendous, but I had to ride it out. I promised myself I would never make another attempt on taking my life, even though I wanted to. I suppose feeling like shit is better than not feeling at all. Was that Eckhart Tolle? Na, I think that was just me being optimistic.

My head now filled with the black sludge of depression; I could feel that things were about to get worse. There was a trainwreck coming. It has taken me a long time to recognise the signs of what depression really was and it was a weight that came over my body and mind. It was hard to move in a positive way. It was hard to get out of bed and do anything.

I was taking my meds as per what my doctor prescribed, but they didn't seem to help much. I tried to take the antidepressants, but they made me feel like I was on speed. I didn't like the feeling at all. I took the other meds, the mood stabilisers, they didn't seem to make me feel anything at all so that wasn't too bad. I had one new med that had been added to my artillery and that was an antipsychotic. Should things get out of hand again, I had this weapon of mass destruction that was guaranteed to out me down for the count, relieve the agitation and ensure that I was not going to go on some kind of manic rampage.

Then there was the looking back. I hated it, but those postmortems just kept flooding my mind. The professor in the laughing academy didn't see the trainwreck unfold and neither did I. He knew when he saw me that I had been manic. For me, the lack of sleep and obsession with the numerology should have been obvious signs that all was not well. The flood in my flat and then reading about Noah's flood in the synagogue may have seemed to be coincidental, but as I had learnt from the recent learning, Jews don't believe in coincidence. Yet those things in my fragile state just pushed the mania to a level 4 out of 5 and I was heading for the wall. Once I or anyone is on a force 4 out of 5 mania there is nothing that will stop them except a visit to the house of pain.

Being in denial about my diagnosis and thinking to myself that I didn't have bipolar was just the icing on the cake. This time when I left the hospital (reprogrammed), I had to accept the harsh truth of my diagnosis. If I wanted to avoid any other trips back to the laughing academy, I needed to acknowledge my condition, and treat it with the proper maintenance of meds and pay close attention to how my brain was working. I had to suck it up and accept the reality of my label.

I had to agree with the doctor's diagnosis again prior to my release as they wanted to make sure I understood my condition. It would have been nice to have a 15 minute one-on-one pep talk to prepare me for the outside world again. Something to help. But no. There is a long evaluation. Me versus them. The questions fly at you, and you had better answer correctly if you want to get out. I can understand that. They don't want to keep you any longer than necessary. But they also want to make sure your brain is back to a healthy rotation.

One minute you're manic with a messed-up brain, and the next you're being released, calmer with a new perspective on life, and a clean bill of health. Having your freedom taken away is the worst, and the process that the doctors put you through to bring you down from the mania is not something that happens overnight. They need time to make sure the elevation has calmed down, and that environment is a real leveller. It surely humbles and takes the steam out of your system fast. So, when you see yourself getting close to being released from that place you are on your best behaviour.

I can only say thank you to the doctors for bringing me round once again. I hate to think of where I would have ended up had I not been side-lined. The Rabbi made the right decision to call in the cops. If you have to go, go with a smile, I don't think that is how it happened, but it sure sounds romantic. Enough of the heavy stuff... and thank G-d I'm not Humpty Dumpty. I was depressed but I realised that I had to start putting myself back together again.

CHAPTER 27
Kick-starting My Depressed Brain

My stories and experiences differ from the next bipolar person, but we do share a commonality of soaring highs and brutal depressions that seem to be inescapable.

Looking back, I am lucky that I have survived my experiences both on the manic and depressed side of the pendulum. How quickly I recover from either side of the condition has varied a lot. The first manic episode was one of the worst, and yet years later I still had bad manias because I was triggered and let the anger explode in my mind.

During the long grind of a depression, I would not answer any calls from friends who were just concerned and ringing to see if I am okay. Eventually, I would call them back just so they know I am not feeling great, and to say that I appreciate their call. These close friends do understand that I am not being rude, I am just not in the mood for conversation. I simply just need time to recoil and heal.

If I do manage to get out to the shops, I hope I don't bump into anyone I know. It is not that I am not a social person, it is just that I find it hard to put on a happy face when in reality, I am chronically depressed.

Prior to my first mania and depression, if I went shopping, I would never look at the price of the groceries or items I wanted to buy. Now things have turned around and I was claiming sickness benefits from the government. I had paid plenty of tax during my working years until then, so I had no guilty feelings in receiving this money.

It amazes me how unwell my mind was during those dark days. I recall thinking that I could live on this limited amount of money for the rest of my life. What I really should have been doing was thinking about finding a job so that I could get back to earning money for myself. I suppose it's not that easy to be positive when you're in a depressed state of mind.

To start my business at 25, build it up for the next five years, only to later watch it implode, was soul destroying on its own. Having to deal with this and the reality of my diagnosis, was a double whammy. The stigma of mental illness was not pleasant either. People can be harsh and judgemental, thinking that I had brought it all on myself. Well, what would they know? Sweet F.A.! I was the only one who had to work out my path to recovery. I had time to research, and I could join some online groups as the internet started becoming an interesting place where anyone could find answers about anything.

And the slow crawl back to being able to work. I think it was not so much that I didn't want to work, I just could not face having to go into a corporate environment and do what I love, which was selling. Firstly, selling is an artform, and secondly if I was feeling badly inside, I could not simply put on a happy face and pretend all is going great in my life. I think it would be easier if I just told whoever was in front of me that I have severe depression and anxiety right now. Can we cut to the chase and just sign the purchase order? Could you just help me out and buy this service please?

The length of time it took me to get better varied a lot. If I found myself being red-carded into the nut farm, well that would be four weeks' time out to start with, and most of the time, after getting out from the puzzle factory, I was in a depressed state of mind. I could not bear the thought of facing people, especially in a corporate office.

In the past, the healing has taken months, if not longer. Apart from adjusting and taking the correct meds as prescribed by my psych doctor, the second most important thing is to set myself small, realistic, easy goals for me to do. If I am in a depressed state, even the task of taking a shower can seem impossible.

One the best things I need to do is push myself to get out of the house for a walk. This also may sound easy, but it is not. My depressed mind would rather have me lie in bed all day, flooding my mind with negative thoughts. As much as I would like to lie in bed and hide when I have been in an extremely down mood, I know that I have to get up eventually, even if it's only to use the bathroom. Once up, I have to fight the negative voice and overcome any excuses that this negative voice throws at me. It is a battle against myself for sure, and if I fail to get out of the house, it's not the end of the world, and I don't give myself a hard time. I obviously need more time and mental strength to beat the negative voice. Should I not be successful in getting out of the house, then I simply say to myself, *'Okay, today you're not going, but tomorrow you are, no excuses'.*

Getting some sunshine in my eyes, and moving my body is not the hard part. Winning the mental game to do the small tasks I set is. Just because I know what I should be doing, doesn't mean it is easy to actually do it. Mentally, I have to

BIPOLAR HEAD

beat the negative thoughts in me, and take it one small goal at a time. In setting my walking goals, I don't set a distance or any length of time, I just promise myself that I am going to get out of the house and get moving. I know that going for a short 15-minute walk is going to make all the difference and give me a sense of achievement that I have done the task. Once I have been able to do this, I know I can go again the next day and the day after that.

It is amazing how easily the negative inclinations in my mind can be the boss. Not fulfilling the goal or task that I have set for the following day makes this negative influence the winner, but only for today. Tomorrow gives me the opportunity to start afresh and if I do get out for my walk, I become the winner.

CHAPTER 28
BDI Pty Ltd

If you recall, in 1989, when I had that horrific year with the marijuana cultivation bust, I mentioned I was working for the third largest computer company in the USA at the time, called AST. This tech company was started by three clever engineers who built their first product, a card that slotted into one of the two free slots of the IBM PC. The product was a Printed Circuit Board (PCB) and had a clock, battery backup and a second parallel port. They sold thousands of these. Then they made other board level products. There were memory boards to expand the amount of RAM in your PC, and they had another line of comms products, when plugged into the IBM PC, it allowed the user to be able to toggle between the mainframe or minicomputer and their desktop. Later, they also brought out their own range of PCs which took them to the heights of success.

IBM didn't really think that their PC was going to become the household item that it is today and didn't even bother to write the operating system for their PC. They just preferred to outsource this to one clever entrepreneur techie called Bill Gates, who developed the DOS operating system, or had some code cutters write it for him, and he licensed this operating system not only to IBM but other PC manufactures who built clone PCs.

Why IBM didn't buy the software outright, I have no idea, but that software was a huge win for Microsoft and put them on a path to becoming the massive company it is today. IBM's mainframe and mini mainframes required a dedicated monitor, so for people who were working on the big systems and had a PC they would need to have two monitors on their desk.

AST built another range of communication PCBs. They were much more powerful than the PC with serious grunt power. There was also a range called the AS400. My job in the company was a sales support role for the computer dealers around Australia. They wanted information on these products, and I would also handle sales. I worked hard to learn about these products and enjoyed it. If I didn't know the answers, I needed to ask the guys in the technical support area for help. But I learnt fairly quickly, and soon I didn't need so much of their help.

The company also printed brochures with technical specs, so I read and reread, and finally picked the information up. One day, a call came in which was about to change my life. This man asked me if I had any memory boards. I said, 'Sure how may would you like?'

He said, 'I will take the lot.'

Dubiously, I asked, 'Mmm, really?'

I knew we had a lot of stock, but I needed some time for the warehouse to get back to me with the exact numbers. I told him I would check the stock levels and get back to him with the units on hand and the price for the lot. This guy was not one of our authorised dealers, he didn't have an account with us which meant the only way we would supply him is if he did a direct payment by bank deposit. Frankly, I thought he was full of shit. I rang him back and I told him how many we had in the warehouse, and it was going to be eighty thousand dollars.

'Would you still like them all?' I asked.

'Yes.'

I almost fell off my chair. That was a big order. I told him that because he didn't have an account with us, he needed to deposit the money into the bank account and send me a fax with the receipt so that I could get the order processed and ready for him. Sure enough, an hour later the fax machine started buzzing and in came the bank receipt for eighty thousand dollars.

In the office they thought I was a hero for doing this sale, but it was easy. He just wanted what we had. I was pleased to get the recognition from my boss, but I wanted to know more about this man and his business. When I had the order processed, I rang him back and thanked him. I also told him we would ship his stock out the following day. I asked for his company details, and he gave me his address. His office was in Bondi Junction which was on my way home. I told him I lived in the east and he offered, 'Why don't you swing past my office, and we can meet?' 'I'd love to,' I agreed.

I can't tell you what day it was, but I remember it being a hot summer's afternoon. When I got to his office, he only had two staff working for him. I was surprised by this, I thought he would have more staff. He showed me his marketing material which was an A4 laminated page with four products on one side and four on the other. Each product had a picture and product description.

He would mail these off once a month to his extensive client base and this marketing worked really well for him, he had a great business.

He asked me how often my company brought in the memory boards.

I told him, 'Probably every two months.'

He said, 'Great! My main business is RAM, as in computer memory chips.' The company I worked for didn't sell the RAM, just the boards that the RAM would slot into. He said, 'When you have other dealers ring in for these memory boards, send them to me. I will sell them the boards, and the memory and give you some commission.'

I didn't have a problem with that. Little did I know I had just met my future business partner. I started to go to his office every day after work. I would sit with him, and he would run off the sales and show me his turnover and daily profit. I was amazed to see just how much he was turning over and what his daily profits were. On a slower day, he would make at least ten thousand dollars. On a great day he would make a forty thousand dollar profit. In a day!

After about three weeks, I told him that I would like to set up a business with him selling a range of AST board products. I approached the CEO of AST and pitched him a plan of how I would go about marketing and selling their computer board level products if he would grant me permission to be a reseller of these products.

The following day I was full of nerves. I wanted this break so badly. The thought of finally having my own business was blowing up inside my head. I just tried to calm my mind and think positively. The morning went by so slowly, and I kept busy, answering calls from our dealers. I couldn't help thinking that if I was granted this opportunity, I would be on the other end of the phone placing the orders.

Lunchtime passed by, and I was finally asked by his secretary to come to his office. I walked in and the boss asked me to take a seat across from him. We had some small talk and he asked me how the day's sales were going. How are the orders today? I told him that we had some good orders come in and he was pleased. He then asked me, 'Are you sure this is what you would like to do? I am considering you for a position in the sales team.'

I told him that I really appreciated that, but my heart was set on going out on my own and focusing on and starting a business with Greg as my business partner and mentor. I didn't want to say this to the boss, but I would always see the guys in the sales team when they were in the office between client visits. My desk was in the sales area and I was seated near to these guys. There was a whiteboard on the wall with their sales targets and actual sales to date. I also heard them talk about the pressures of having to constantly bring in the business. Selling computers in 1989 was a very competitive business. It was a stressful job, but these guys were sales assassins, most of them managed to hit their budgets, and when they did, the booze would be on for all in the boardroom most Friday afternoons.

I saw it as a high-pressure job, and I knew what I wanted, and that was to learn all I could from Greg. His business was going gangbusters, and he was also an excellent sales guy as well. Meanwhile, I think the constant pressure of being in a tight and competitive sales team was not something that I cared for. If you did have a good month, as soon as the month ended, you were into a new month and the pressure started all over again.

The sales guys were mainly selling the PCs and servers. I knew from the conversations I'd heard that they were always under pressure to meet their KPI's, and sales targets. The sales team consisted of four sales guys who had dealers and clients from all over the country. They also travelled interstate frequently. I'd had enough of travel when touring around Australia with the bands I played in. I had spent a year learning about the other products AST had, and that is what I wanted to focus on.

The boss asked one more time, 'Are you sure you want to be a sub-distributor for our board level products?'

I said, 'Very much so.'

With that he then said, 'Congratulations! I will get my secretary to give you the forms to fill out and I wish you all the best. Good luck.'

I thanked him and left his office in the best mood. I rang Greg and told him the good news. He also congratulated me and told me to come by the office on my way home, 'Let's go grab a beer to celebrate.'

I left AST at the end of the week and began working on my own marketing page of products from the AST range. It took me two days to get the product range right and when I did, Greg asked me to come with him to the printer who was a lovely guy called Ray. Ray asked me to double check the spelling and wording for the artwork and then he would show me the mockup before finally going to print.

Now that that was underway, I needed to work out where I was going to set my business up and run it from. I asked my father if I could set up my business from one of the rooms at the back of his photography studio. It was such an exciting time for me. I had no idea about how to run a business or what I needed to do. I didn't even know what an invoice was, but that was all part of my crash course in business 101. I decided to make Greg my 5050 partner. In hindsight, I should have taken a larger percentage, even 1-percent more. After all, I was doing all the work, but Greg did fund the business to start with. I was naive and green, but so thrilled to get things going.

It took a couple of weeks to get organised with my little office, buying two desks, and getting the 4-line Commander telephone system in place. I had a sign made up for the front of the studio to hang under my father's business sign. Dad's business was called Parisian Studios. He had a large sign out the front with his business name and logo which was the Eiffel Tower. I had my business name and logo attached underneath. I had to choose a business name and I decided on Board Distributors International, BDI Pty Ltd for short. It was a catchy name, and Ray's graphic guy came up with a cool black and red logo which looked great. I was so excited. Of course, I had business cards made up with my title as Managing Director. I never knew how I was going to start my own business, and I was so excited that this was my time to get started. I was 26 and ready to get into starting this business.

Finally, the day came, and my marketing material was ready to be mailed out to Greg's database of about twenty thousand potential customers. There were government and computer dealers, as well as large corporate companies. It was a good mix of potential clients. Greg took his database very seriously and had one of his staff spend most of her week maintaining it. Constantly adding names and updating the information to ensure the right person was going to receive the marketing material.

Everything was in place and the marketing went out. From the first week, I had calls coming in with people either placing orders or wanting to know more about the products. As the orders came in, I would in turn order product from AST, drive over to their warehouse and pick up the stock.

In my first month, I turned over eighty thousand dollars at 40-percent margin. It was a great start. At the end of the month Greg came over to my office, his office was not far away, about five hundred metres. Greg sat down and asked me how I was enjoying working for myself and I told him I was loving it. He then asked me to show him the invoices from my first month's sales in the business. I asked him, 'What's an invoice?'

Greg explained what an invoice was, and how I need to include an invoice with every order I sent out. He asked, 'If you haven't been writing up an invoice how have you been tracking the sales and customer names?'

I told him I was writing each order down into a cash receipts book. The first page went with the goods to the customers who all had to pay upfront before I would ship the goods out. Then there was a carbon copy in the book for my record. He then told me to buy a PC from AST.

'I will load some accounting software on it for you. When the stock comes in, you enter the stock into the package and when you make a sale, you can print off an invoice for the client and the software will keep a record of your sales per item as well as your profit and loss statements.'

It was a bit of a steep learning curve, but I was off and running.

By the end of the year, I had turned over eight hundred thousand dollars. It was a brilliant start; I could not have been happier. In my second year, all seemed to be going even better. I was on track to grow my business by at least 40-percent. Then my business partner, Greg, ordered two AST 486 servers from me. I had a credit account with AST, and each server cost twenty thousand dollars. I had 30 days to pay them. When I got the servers, I sold them to Greg at cost and gave him 14 days to pay me the forty thousand dollars. Not making money on the deal was fine, but I should have asked him for the forty thousand on delivery.

During the same month, I had also sold fifty thousand dollars' worth of AST product to a government department in Canberra. The profit was lean as I had to supply the items at a very competitive price. It just so happened that in the same week I was sent a dealer memo from AST which said that if I sold any product to government, I was entitled to an additional 10-percent discount on these items. This meant I would get another five thousand dollars profit back from AST.

I rang them up to discuss getting my 10-percent rebate, and they asked me to come into their office for a meeting. Later that week, I went to their office, and I met with the managing director and marketing manager to discuss the rebate on the sale that I made. In the meeting, they said they were not going to give me the additional money back which I thought was unfair, but then as a sweetener they did offer me their full range of computers and servers to add onto the other products I was already selling. I liked that, but I still didn't agree with them on not giving me the money that I believed I was entitled to. After discussing these points, I could not believe what was to follow.

From left field, they dropped a bomb on me. There was one other condition, they wanted me to split my business, so Greg was no longer my business partner. They then said some very unflattering things about him and began dishing the dirt on Greg. Apparently, Greg had a bit of a bad reputation from a company he owned and ran previously in Melbourne. Greg had purchased some stock from Toshiba. Maybe I should be more precise, he got about a hundred thousand dollars' worth of stock from Toshiba and he never paid his bill. In a way it was a very crazy time in the business, with many companies not honouring their clients' orders, it was a bit like the wild west.

The company Greg started and ran in Melbourne was going really well. He had ten sales guys and admin, and he really was kicking arse. DRAM (Dynamic Random Access Memory) is the last component that goes into a computer. It is last because it is the most expensive and sometimes hard to get, but like the CPU, the price fluctuated a lot, and so large computer manufacturers who had clients like Greg decided that they were not going to supply these outstanding orders. Who could blame them? The price of DRAM went from $2.50 a chip up to $30 a chip. That's right, an obscene hike in price due to no supply. The manufacturers were not going to supply Greg with such a crazy shortage, and of course were going to do what everyone else did; jack the prices up and take advantage of these market conditions. Why should they fulfil outstanding orders to companies like Greg's and have him make a fortune? No, they decided to do it themselves and let the little guys go to the wall.

When Greg could not get any stock, and he had orders with several of the manufacturers, his company had nothing to trade. He had orders in with manufacturers such as NEC, Toshiba and Mitsubishi, who would not honour these orders even though the order price per unit was written clearly on the purchase order. Suing them wasn't going to work as Greg needed cashflow or he wasn't going to have a company. He needed stock to sell so he could keep his business afloat. Greg was in a bind, and that doesn't mean you just grab what you can and run, but he got screwed and lied to, and I doubt a hundred thousand dollars would even be a scratch for a company like Toshiba. Not long after that, his company hit the wall.

I had not heard this story before. However, I didn't like them trash talking about my business partner, I left the meeting not knowing what to think or tell Greg. In my innocent naive way, I decided to spill the beans. I went over to Greg's office and told him what they said. He lit up and became enraged. Greg said, 'Screw those guys! You're not doing business with them anymore.'

I couldn't believe what I was hearing. I said, 'Greg, my whole product range is all AST, if I don't have their product for sale, I don't have a business.'

'I don't care, you're done with them! Go find some other products to sell.'

He was enraged, 'I'm going to sue those guys for defamation as well.'

I hit the floor. 'Greg, you can't do that, I've worked for these guys for well over a year, this is not cool.'

He didn't care what I had to say, his mind was made up. 'Nobody is going to get away with defaming me. Oh, and by the way I am not paying for the two servers I bought from you either.'

I said, 'Greg, well technically you didn't buy them from me. I gave you credit for those boxes, which I owe forty thousand dollars on. You can't be serious?' Oh, he was serious.

'No f-ing way I am going to pay.'

I pleaded with him, 'Please! You can't do this to me.'

He just said, 'Screw those f-ckers! And you just get on with looking for a new product range to sell.'

I looked at him wearily and said, 'Sure. Why don't I just go to Coles and take a long stroll down the computer networking aisle and see what I can find? Mate, seriously I know you're pissed off, but we are doing well with their products. Why do you have to take this so personally?'

'Why? Why? I will tell you why. It is a matter of my name that's why.'

'And what about my name?' I replied, 'I have done no wrong. And if I hadn't of told you this, I would not be arguing with you about this right now.'

'Well lucky for me, you're honest and you stuck up for me!' He shouted back.

I said, 'Yeah that's right. But it doesn't mean you have to sabotage my business!'

All he said was, 'Don't worry, you will be fine. You will find other products out there.'

Holy crap! I was in disbelief. What was I going to do? Greg was scary when he was in this mood. His mind was made up, and it was bad luck for me. Why did I have to open my big mouth. Sometimes I am just too honest.

Just start looking for other products to sell…

Far out, why? I love selling the products in my range now! I was sick to the core. My whole business was about to come crashing to a halt. I knew what was going to happen next and it did. I didn't need to be Nostradamus. Surprise, surprise, the nasty demand letters for money came rolling in. AST started sending me letters of demand for the two servers Greg bought or should I say ordered and took from me. He was like a bull with a red flag, and there was no way he was going to pay for those machines. I didn't like what was going down at all. I owed them forty thousand dollars. They also stopped supplying me all the other products that I was selling for them, so effectively I was screwed.

I went from having a business doing well to being thrown into suspended animation. The relationship with AST was over. I owed them the money, but they also got the lawsuit that Greg had hammered them with. He was hitting them up for a hundred thousand dollars in damages. I thought he was crazy.

Suddenly, I had a lot of time on my hands, and I tried finding a new product line, but it was not easy. Meanwhile I had legal letters flying in. I had never experienced anything like this before. AST sued me for the money I owed them, which was fair enough. Greg owed me that money, and there was no way he was going to give me a cent. I was stuck. I had some money in the bank, but I wasn't going to pay the bill without Greg's consent.

The thought of having to go to court and being wound up made me ill. Where were the simple good old days of this business? It wasn't that far away, I was selling product, and making bank. Everything was going so well and then BOOM it all turned to steam.

I knew nothing of the legal process, and I didn't want to find out. Greg on the other hand, loved it. He used some lawyers in his building. They seemed to think he was in with a good chance. The threat of legal action from them just made me ill. I didn't want to have anything to do with it. They wanted their money back, which was never going to happen now, and I thought back to how this all started.

If only they would have given me that extra commission. I would not have been going through all of this. I was young, and so intimidated by Greg, and he was my business partner, so I had to do as he said. In the back of my mind, I was also scared he was going to sue me as well, should I try and sort it out or pay them so much as a dollar. No, he was like a dog with a bone on this one, he loved it and he really thought he was going to make money out of it.

So sure enough, Greg countersued them, and when the matter went to court, Greg won the defamation case, to the tune of a hundred thousand dollars in damages, and a formal apology. I have no idea why the servers never had to be paid for, maybe he got those as a sweetener for not suing the MD of the company personally. I could not believe it. Well, he certainly taught me a lesson there. In fact, I learnt a huge lesson that day, never be intimidated or pushed around by the big guy. Unless of course it's a street fight, then you run.

This all happened over a six-month period. While it was easy for Greg to go and find some new products, I had nothing on my radar, and it was looking grim. I was now desperately looking for products to sell and couldn't find anything. The money in my bank account was dwindling and I think I was down to my last seven thousand dollars. The phones had stopped ringing, except for friends of course and it was doom and gloom for my business. I honestly thought this was going to be the last legs of BDI and I hated it. I was a few weeks away from being down and out.

Then, one afternoon I just happened to walk outside to the front of the studio, and I saw two Chinese guys standing there, holding one of my A4 laminated product sheets. They were right in front of the shop, with a very confused look on their faces, as they were trying to find my business but didn't come inside to the waiting room. Lucky for me, I noticed my product marketing sheet, and I asked if I could help them. They asked if I knew where BDI was, and I said that it was my business and asked how I could help them.

They told me they were from Taiwan and were representing a manufacturer of computer networking products. Their line of products was like the products I used to distribute for AST, and they even had more products that they copied from other manufacturers.

At that moment I could not believe my luck. I rang Greg and told him to come meet us at the coffee shop around the corner from his office. We arrived at the coffee shop and five minutes later Greg walked in to join us. During our meeting these gentlemen told us that they were looking to sign up another distributor for Australia. They already had two wholesale distributors selling their product range and they wanted a third. They pulled out some of their marketing material and I could not believe what I saw. Their company made identical products to the well known American made products, but they were about 50-percent cheaper.

This was unbelievable, and the timing incredible as well. I will never forget one of the gentleman's name. His name was Titus Song. Unique right? Well, just like that my prayers had been answered and I had a range of products to sell. I got down to the task of making up the new marketing material and it was at the printers three days later ready to be printed.

I had a new line of 12 products ready to go. As soon as the A4 laminated product sheets were printed, I had them sent to the mailing house so that they could stuff them into envelopes and distribute the marketing product sheets to our client base. Once they were mailed out, it was only a matter of time, and the phones were going to start ringing like before. A few days later, bingo! I was back in business. A few months went by, and I had managed to really turn things around. By the end of my second year, I had a turnover of 1.2 million dollars.

I forgot to mention that Greg was also a huge gambler. He owned about eight racehorses. He also loved to fly up to the casino on the Gold Coast and play Baccarat. One Friday he came into my office and said he wanted me to take out thirty thousand dollars from the company bank account as he was heading to the casino. I tried to argue it out with him, but it was impossible. He just swore at me and said, 'Just f-ing do it!'

So, I did. Off he went that Friday night. The following week, I was so pissed off, I decided if he was going to take a dollar or thirty thousand dollars out, so was I. I had always loved Porches so; it was time to do a little shopping. The following week I found one for sale for twenty-eight thousand dollars and bought it. What's good for the goose is good for the other goose. Greg was so pissed off, but I couldn't care less. I then spent another ten thousand dollars on it, rebuilding the engine. Business was good. We were making money, but if I had some more sense, I would have put a deposit on another property.

In my third year, I ended up turning over 1.8 million dollars, in year four I turned over 2.2 million dollars. Year five was my great collapse. I had by then separated from Greg who wanted me to pay him sixty thousand dollars to buy him out. That was a lot of coin. I didn't know what to do. I wanted to keep the client base that I had and built up and I didn't want to cut and run as he would have for sure sued me, so I told him, 'Why don't you buy me out for sixty thousand?'

I had done all the hard work in that business, and had I just had 51 percent, I would have been in a better position to fight with him. I knew that if I tried to just take the business and cut and run, he would have sued me for sure. In the end I settled with him and paid him twenty-five thousand dollars to buy him out.

There were some other complications. Greg had moved into a large office space and had me move my business in there to share some of his overhead. So, I needed to find an office to work from. Little did I know that later that year my marriage was about to go and so was my business followed by my mind as I was now 31, and that is when I had my first psychosis. Yes, I was about to have that long night up followed by the chat on the beach.

So ended BDI, and my life as a businessman. It was brutal. But obviously that was my destiny and fate. Looking back though it was a great five-year run. The money came and went. I was obviously not a good custodian of it. With the money I spent on that Porsche, I should have put a deposit down on a house.

Would'a, Could'a, Should'a.

I suppose back then I thought I didn't want to be an old man in a Porsche, and always thought to myself that if I was going to own a Porsche I wanted one as a younger man. These days I drive a Toyota Corolla Hybrid and I love it. Oh, what a feeling! I did have a lot of fun in that Porsche. But it was only a car. There are more important things in life, such as your health.

CHAPTER 29
Sell That Bandwidth 1997

It was 1997, I had time back in the laughing academy and I was back in the house of D. The depression once again consumed my mind. It is a brutal master or cruel mistress. Take your pick. I won't discriminate; it certainly doesn't. It just swoops in and takes over our brains and souls and eats away at us indiscriminately. It takes everything in your power to get rid of. It is draining and stops us from being our best selves. It sucks the life out of us like a parasite. So please, if you're suffering with this condition, do everything you can to be well and stay in the game, number one. Number two, be good to yourself. I can't say that enough. We are all here for a reason. It would be nice if we had that clearly marked out; *Here is your life planned out, now go for it! You're going to become this amazing person, you'll grow from a little baby, into a wonderful human.* But that is the mystery road that we all travel down. I have learnt that there is only one thing, and that is do more good things than bad. The rest are just hurdles to overcome. Ignore the negative, thrive on the positive.

So, it's 1997. I was coming out of a bad depression, and I saw an ad in the paper for a sales role with an internet company. In fact, this company was an Internet Service Provider (ISP). I am not going to give the company name to protect the innocent or not so innocent.

I went to meet with the recruiter, and I found out this was a young, up-and-coming corporate ISP, and they were doing well. They had the largest newspaper in the country host their website with them, and they focused solely on corporate business. I went in to meet with the sales manager. When I got to the office it was a smallish space with about thirty-five people working there. They were all young. In fact, the average age was 25, and that included the managing director.

I was 32 at the time and I had a good interview. The sales manager was also a young man of 25, who offered me the role right away.

'We are looking for people to start ASAP, when can you come on board?'

I said, 'I can start Monday.'

It was Thursday, and I needed a few days to adjust to the fact that I was going to be back in the 'slave to the rhythm' of the corporate grind. That was okay, I was still young enough to give this a go and had to. I had nothing else at home except boring hours of TV and the occasional book to read. The recruiter rang me and said, 'Please come in tomorrow so we can sign the paperwork and negotiate your salary.'

The following day I went to see her, and I agreed to a number plus commission, and I signed my work rights away. Let the games begin.

I enjoyed my last weekend; I got my corporate wear dusted off and I was pleased I could still fit into a suit. All that eating during depression may have put on a few pounds, but I was still able to squeeze into my pants and jacket. I was very keen to buy a new suit once I got my pay packet – it was time to look a bit sharper.

I caught the bus and train into work on my first day and walked into the open-plan office. It was a brash new company, young and full of enthusiasm. That's fine. As the oldest guy on the floor, I came with no reputation. That was about to be made.

I was introduced around, and I think after the fourth or fifth person, I could not remember another name. It was not my strong point. But I was not there for a social and I was certainly not there to make friends. I was given a desk, and about two desks behind me was a wall with a whiteboard attached to it. It had all the sales guys' names on it. Naturally it was in descending order one through to six. I was the seventh sales guy to join the team. I am not sure why there were no women on the list. Maybe this place was just a home for sales cowboys. I found out in time that it was.

I think it took about a month for me to get my head around the company's products, and by month two I was already on top of the sales leaderboard. We had to cold call all our sales. No marketing for this company. It was hard but honest hunting. I loved that part. It was always great getting a sale, but the hunting was challenging. It was the early days of the internet, so everyone wanted bigger connectivity and we were the company that had the pipes to deliver.

We were one of the first companies to have DSL, or ADSL which was a delivery method. To be able to deliver that service the client had to be within 6 kilometres of the POP or access point. As we focused on clients mainly in the city it wasn't too bad.

The environment of that company was almost like a mini version of *The Wolf of Wall Street*. Thursday nights were mandatory drinking and cocaine nights, with a must show up for work policy on Friday. That didn't stop people from getting on it on other days, and as for the merry-go-round of who was sleeping with who, well that seemed to be a bit of a free for all. I was too old for that and didn't get involved with anyone at the office. Besides, I wanted a Jewish woman, and sadly there were none of those working in the company.

I have to say it was a crazy place to work and if there was anything good that came out of it, it was the friendship I made with the most handsome man in the universe. Well, that was my nickname for him. He managed to shag his way around the office, and had a bevy of women in the time that I knew him.

We are still good mates today. I reacquainted myself with him about 10 years after I left the company. I know today he lives a clean life away from the booze and drugs, off-grid somewhere in Southern Queensland near a pickle farm. I affectionately refer to him as the pickle farmer. I don't think he minds. But I adore him as a friend and sober buddy I can call my mentor. When I went into the AA programme he helped me a lot, especially after my first mentor turned into a prick fascist. He did get me to three months sober, then I managed to go the rest of the way without his help. But I did enlist the pickle farmer to help me.

But back to the company. It was about a year and a half that I managed to stay with this mob. I was promoted to sales manager after a year, and while all the other young guns drove their shiny new 911's, I was still in my Honda Civic. The sales manager that was our boss before I was promoted was a right prick.

I can say that because he was. I am not dropping names, but he put me under a ridiculous amount of pressure. He rode me hard to get the results out of the guys, and it was not great as I had been one of the boys in the team, and now I found myself to be their boss. They didn't really reward me with much incentive either, so after a brief period of a few months, I started looking around for a new job.

I eventually found that new job and handed in my resignation. A few months later the ISP had a new major investor and not long after that the company also listed on the Australian Stock Exchange. They became the darling of the stock market, and their shares went ballistic. Should I have hung around? Maybe, maybe not. I can't deal with BS. If they offered me some kind of decent remuneration I probably would have hung around.

Just shy of two years with the ISP, I found a company which was an Israeli software developer. Little did I know, I had met my future partner in crime.

CHAPTER 30
A Little Bit Of Magic

The Israeli company had a product which was called Magic. It was a software tool that allowed you to write code and deploy the software onto multiple platforms. I was interviewed by an Israeli gentleman called Avi. He was a likeable person but totally dyslexic, as I was to find out later.

He had a business partner who was away at the time but when he got back, we hit it off like a house on fire. Needless to say, I got the job, quit the ISP and was happy to see the end of my workdays there.

I started with Magic and went on a few sales calls with Avi. Sadly, he was hopeless with these sales meetings, and I had no success in closing any deals. When his business partner came back, it was a whole different ballgame. His name was Mike Ronson. Mike and I would go to sales meetings and worked so well together we just could not lose.

I loved going to sales meetings with Mike because no matter what companies we went to see, they would always have their technical person on hand to ask questions and Mike had all the answers. He was a code cutter himself, or should I say he was a systems architect. He could write a billing system for a major telco, he was that bright. How those two met, I have no idea, but Mike and I went on the sales calls together and we managed to close some good business deals.

Six months had passed, and I was enjoying working there, but then one day I came to work, and Avi told me that he and Mike had split. I was shattered. It was not good for me as I would now rather go on sales meetings alone than go on sales calls with Avi, that would be sales suicide.

So, I went on some more calls and then decided to go on calls by myself. If I was presented with technical questions that I could not answer, I would let the potential client know I would get back to them with the answers.

It was a difficult time for me. The year was 1999, and my father was sadly suffering with cancer and didn't have long to go. My mother was looking after him at home and I was not sure if she was giving him the right amount of pain medication, he just always seemed to be in agony. Eventually, he sadly passed away, and my twelve-month period of mourning period began. I loved my father. He was the funniest man I knew. I couldn't stand watching him wither away, in one way I was relieved that he was no longer suffering.

In the Jewish world it is the obligation of the son to say Kaddish (Mourner's prayer) for his parents. I was still very new to the world of Orthodox Judaism. When you are given a Torah education you learn about the Jewish High Holy Days and customs, and how to live a Torah life. I only had a reform Sunday school education. It didn't make my parents nor me any less Jewish than the next person. At the end of the day, no human being can see the soul of a person, so who are we to judge who is a holier person than the next? Of course, there are times when us Jews had leaders who were connected to G-d in a very special way. The last being the Rebbe who sadly passed away in the early '90s.

On my father's passing, I tried to do the right thing and I went to synagogue for morning and afternoon/evening services to say Kaddish in honour of my father. Saying Kaddish can only be said when there is a quorum of ten men. There is no mention of death in this prayer, only a glorification of G-d's name, but when a son says this prayer twice a day it elevates the soul during the transition period from this world to the next. My preference for services was the Yeshiva Synagogue on Flood Street. Little did I know that my life again was about to change for the better.

CHAPTER 31
Opportunity Knocks Again

One day while I was at *shul* (synagogue) on Flood Street in Bondi for morning prayers, a gentleman approached me and asked me if I was saying Kaddish for my father. He introduced himself as Abraham Schwartz and said, 'Please, call me Abe.'

He knew my dad well and told me that my father had taken his wedding photos. He wished me a long life, as is customary and then said, 'I believe you work in the computer industry.'

I said, 'Yes.'

He then asked if I could go to his office to have a meeting with him. I had no idea what this was all about, but agreed to go to his office which was in the city. I found the building where he worked and hopped into the lift to the 8th floor. I walked in and announced myself to the receptionist stating that I had an appointment with Mr Schwartz. She rang him and had a brief chat after which she asked me to take a seat. Five minutes later, a door opened and out came Mr Schwartz. I greeted him with a cordial, 'Good Morning Mr Schwartz!'

He said, 'Please, call me Abe, everyone calls me Abe.'

I followed Abe and we walked in to his office which had a lovely view of the park below and busy street action. The office had an open-plan layout, and his companies occupied the whole floor. There may have been 30 people working there and everyone seemed to be going about their business. We sat down in his office and Abe explained to me that he was the chairman of two public companies. One was a gold mining company, the other was a nickel mining company. He told me that the gold mining company wanted to invest into various IT projects.

The dot-com space in IT was exploding all around the world and while gold was in a quiet phase for now, he and his business associates were looking at taking a different direction. Modestly, he told me that there was plenty of money in the bank and while he was not going to take massive risks, he was prepared to explore business opportunities in the dot-com space.

With all of that laid out on the table I asked the obvious question, 'So how can I help you, Abe?'

'Before we continue, may I ask you a personal question?' He asked.

I said, 'Certainly.'

Abe asked if I had put on *tefillin* that day. I told him I did, and this put a smile on his face. I told him it is my spiritual medication. I explained to him my story briefly without going into too much detail. I told him that I had only put on *tefillin* for the first time at the age of 31, after I had a serious health issue. At this point I was unsure if I should tell him about my bipolar disorder. I was very guarded with who I told and who I didn't tell. But I felt very reassured that he was not only a man with Torah principles, but he was also non-judgemental. I just had a gut feeling as well that I was dealing with someone who was honest, and he approached me, so therefore he had the right to know first-hand. Besides, as he was a regular at the Yeshiva Synagogue, it would have taken him about 10 minutes on the phone to find out about my past, as it was the worst kept secret in the Jewish community.

Abe then said, 'Thank you for sharing that with me,' he then continued, 'may I give you some advice?'

'Of course,' I said.

Abe said, 'With mental health, people do not understand. Even the doctors have limited knowledge,' to which I agreed.

He then said, 'Thank you for sharing. Most people will not be as sympathetic as me. They even may use this against you and discriminate towards you, so best keep it to yourself.'

I agreed. He was right on the money, and to this day, that has been some of the best advice anyone has given me.

Then Abe said, 'May Hashem bless you on your path of Yiddishkeit, and may he bless you and provide you with health and *parnossa* and only good things!'

For a moment I wondered if Abe was a Rabbi, he certainly had the customary long beard, was dressed in a smart suit and tie, and had *tzitzits* hanging from his waist. He had the wisdom and advice, followed with a *bracha*. It made me wonder who was this man with the gentle voice giving me wonderful life advice?

Abe stood up from his desk, asked me if I'd like a drink, to which I declined. He said, 'Please follow me.'

We walked down the corridors of his office. There were some people there who were also religious Jews who I had seen at Yeshiva, busy working away. We walked into the boardroom and there on the table were some large rocks. I picked one up, and Abe asked me if I had ever seen nickel before. I told him I had not.

'Well, the rock you are holding in your hand is nickel, and that is what my other company is mining.'

Of course, mining wasn't the reason Abe asked me to meet with him. I noticed at the end of the large boardroom table there were two piles of papers each about a foot high. Abe asked me to have a look at them and excused himself as he had some phone calls to take care of.

'Please come back to my office once you have had a look at these proposals.'

Abe left the boardroom, and I pulled up a chair and started at the top of the pile, working my way down. As I progressed through the documents, I found it fascinating. I realised that Abe was a well-connected businessman as most of the proposals were from Israel, some from the USA, but how did he manage to get so many companies to send him their investment deck, or fundraising documents?

I looked at these documents and they were all proposals from companies who were looking for investors. I got about three quarters of the way down the first pile, and I had to stop. I know Abe wanted me to go through all of them, but I didn't want to waste his time. I walked back to his office, he was on the phone, I thought he may have been speaking Hungarian at first, but he had no accent when he spoke English. Then I realised he was talking Yiddish. Now there is a language that I would love to be able to speak, but it's almost a forgotten language, used mainly by Chassidic Jews.

Abe motioned for me to sit down, and I did. He gave me the oneminute salute and not long after he finished his call, he asked me, 'So, what do you think?'

I asked him, 'What would you like me to do for you and your company?'

He said, 'I would like you to help our company decide on which ventures are worthy of investing into.'

He explained to me that the price of gold was very flat at that moment, and without being too technical, it would cost them more to mine an ounce of gold at present than what it's worth, so it wasn't worthwhile to extract the gold from the ground at this stage. With that, he told me he had a very wide business network, and it was through this circle of business associates and friends that he came by all of these companies who sent him their proposals for investment.

Then I explained to Mr Schwartz (Abe), that my roles and experience in IT was sales and marketing, but I knew someone that was an excellent technocrat and together we made an excellent team. Abe then stood up and said, 'Great! When can you and your Technocrat come back so I can meet him?'

I told Abe that I would give him a call later in the day to work out a time for the three of us to meet.

'Excellent! I'm looking forward to meeting your guy.'

'You won't be disappointed,' I said, 'Oh and by the way, he is not Jewish.'

Abe said, 'Not everyone is Jewish, Moishe, but just to let you know, I have a business partner that I have worked with for over 20 years, and he is not Jewish. We must never discriminate.'

I said, 'Of course not. I will call you later today.'

So this was the start of my next work opportunity.

I told Mike about the meeting I had with Abe, and he was interested to come and meet with him. A few days later we went to Abe's office and Mike, and I looked over the documents that Abe presented to me the last time I was there. Together Mike and I agreed that we could help Abe with which ventures he should consider. Abe was a generous man and gave us an offer we couldn't refuse. I was delighted at the thought of working with Mike again, and with that I gave notice to Magic.

Mike and I got to work and began sorting out the good proposals from the ones we thought were pie-in-the-sky. The money that some of these companies were asking for was ridiculous especially since none of them had made any money whatsoever. That was the trend back then for most of the companies that were still in development phase yet had the balls to ask for several million dollars for a product they had yet to finish or bring to market.

I loved working with Mr Schwartz and Mike. The office was a great working environment, with *mezuzahs* on all the doorposts. It was also good to have a boss who could teach me some Torah every day. One of the other business partners Abe had, was a genius geologist who could sniff out minerals just by looking at the layout of the land. I knew nothing about how public companies worked and I enjoyed learning about all things mining from Abe and his business partner William.

After a few months of being there, Mike and I had worked our way through the list of proposals. We also spoke to many of these companies to gain further insight into what they were proposing. It wasn't easy but we drew up a shortlist of companies that we now had to really meet with so we could take a closer look at the people behind the scenes and how they intended to bring their products to market.

Some of the companies we were considering were located in Israel. Abe then asked me to join him on a business trip to Israel to meet with these companies. I was over the moon. I was being paid a handsome salary and given stock options, and now I was going on a fully paid business trip to The Holy Land! Mike had some obligations at home, so he stayed behind.

CHAPTER 32
Off To The Promised Land

On this business trip, we were accompanied by another gentleman by the name of Isaac. Both Abe and Isaac were men of Torah values, and devout Lubavitchers. Being in Israel with them was an eye-opening experience. When I was younger and playing music travelling around the country, most of my friends went on a tour of Israel for young people called Academy. I never did this tour but always asked my friends on their return, 'What was Israel like?'

They all simply said, 'You have to go there and experience it yourself.'

After a few days of being there I got it.

Every doorpost had *mezuzahs* on it and just being on the holy ground felt like I had been there before. There was something magical about it. As reincarnation is a fundamental belief in Judaism, I thought to myself, I must have been here before. It was a wonderful experience. I truly loved it. The place was alive, the food was fantastic, and mostly kosher.

Abe, Isaac, and I went to several business meetings, and when it came to having lunch or dinner, Isaac always checked the kosher level of the restaurants we ate at. They had to be what is called 'glatt kosher.' This is the highest level of kosher a restaurant can hold, meaning that the food was not only super kosher, but was guaranteed to block you up big time.

One night in Tel Aviv, I went to retire to my room. I knew that I had a business lunch meeting the next day. I sat in my room, bored, watching Israeli TV in Hebrew, and finally I'd had enough, I just could not stop myself. I had to go out and check out the nightlife. I remember it was a Tuesday night, so I wasn't expecting there to be too much going on. I didn't want Abe to know, he had his room next to mine but that didn't stop me.

I went out to the entertainment and nightclub district. I found a venue called the Barby Club. They had live bands and while I didn't understand what the songs were about, the music was great, and the vibe of the place was fantastic. One of the three bands I saw that night had a drummer with only one arm! He played excellently, in fact all the bands I saw were great.

The night rolled on into the early hours of the morning, and it was now coming up to 6 am. I went back to the Hilton where we were staying, and I thought to myself that I have made it back without Abe from finding out. As I got to the door of my hotel room, I heard Abe's door open, I didn't have enough time to make it inside. I got sprung. Abe was just going down to pray with the *minyan*, and he gave me a, 'Are you just getting home look?'

He didn't really have to ask as he knew, he is an intuitive man and not stupid. He just said, 'Did you have a good time?'

I said, 'Yes, it was great.'

On that note he said he was going to *shul* and told me to get some sleep and be up in a few hours for our meeting.

Darn it! I thought I was going to get away with that one. I was exhausted and entered my room to get a few hours of sleep. I woke up to the sound of knocking on my door. I opened it and it was Abe.

'Come on get ready we have a meeting in 20 minutes.'

I jumped in the shower, got myself scrubbed up and headed down to the restaurant where we met Abe and Isaac. I was so tired, I had a few head nods during the meeting, which was embarrassing, but the product was not exactly exhilarating either. Eventually the meeting ended, and Abe said, 'Go back to your room. You look a bit wrecked.'

I said, 'Yes, too many vodkas & Red Bulls I think.'

So now Abe realised he had employed a party animal. But that was about as far as I could push it. I promised no more sneaking out on school nights. We had been there for about two weeks and seen a lot of companies. I could not decide on any of them as they wanted ridiculous money for a small stake in their businesses. The valuations for these businesses were ridiculous.

Abe and Isaac were now keen to get back to their families as Pesach (Passover) was approaching, but I wanted to stay on. I had found out that there was a computer convention coming up the next week and it would be a good idea to go to the show and see if I could find anything of interest there. Abe agreed, and as their time in The Holy Land came to an end, I was now on my own to venture around and explore the country for myself.

I went on a bus trip to the north of Israel, near the Lebanese border where I spent a night, then headed to Jerusalem which was nothing short of amazing. In Jerusalem, I think one of the saddest things I noticed was the amount of people that were on the streets begging for money. It is a popular lie to say Jews control the banks and money, yet one sad statistic I found out was that 25-percent of the Israeli population was living below the poverty line. This obviously didn't make any sense to me at all. I tried to give money to these street beggars, a few coins here and a few dollars there, it all adds up in the end, but I just could not give as much as I would have liked to.

I had amazing experiences of walking to the Wailing Wall every day to pray and say Kaddish for my dad there. It was still a very emotional time for me, that combined with the excitement of Jerusalem's nightlife. There were so many cool little bars to check out at night, I loved it. There were also numerous nice little *shuls* to go and pray at. I finally understood what my friends meant when they said that you just have to go there and experience Israel for yourself. It is truly a unique place and the Jewish homeland.

Then there was also the tension from the Arabs. As I walked through the market stalls on my way to the Wailing Wall, I felt uncomfortable with some of the looks that I got. I thought to myself that as much as I loved Israel, I could not live there. It was way too intense for me. When I met Israeli's and told them I was from Australia, their faces would light up. They would say, 'Ahh, you come from Australia!'

I think Australians are always well received overseas, and especially so in Israel. I think that Australia is perceived as some magical island in the sun, with the most beautiful beaches and wildlife. That part is true, but there is a darker side to this country, and that fact lies in that it can be a rather racist place. I know that with my Mediterranean looks I was classified as a 'wog' when I was growing up. Not that it bothered me that much. Just don't call me "A F-ing Jew!"

Not many people realise that there are very few Black residents in Australia. This is mainly due to Australia operating under a White Australia Policy which limited the presence of Black individuals, until 1973 when the Labor government finally renounced this and established a policy of multiculturalism. Israel on the other hand did not have any such policies. The country is a real melting pot of cultures.

I ended up going to the computer convention which was fantastic. In total I ended up staying six weeks in The Holy Land. I loved every minute of it and would go back in a heartbeat. The plane ride home was long though and once again I flew via Hong Kong. I didn't get to stay too long there as I felt I had already overstayed my trip, but it was a wonderful experience, and to think I got paid as well, that was a bonus.

I knew that I had told Abe about my bipolar but what I didn't tell him was that I think that I had been feeling manic of late. I was manic and I ended up in a state. This time I was going to head out of town as I didn't want to end up in trouble with the Bondi Police again. So, I decided to up and leave.

CHAPTER 33
Let's Go To Vegas

Lord knows what I was thinking, but I was definitely elevated. I had very little money on me, but enough to buy a one-way ticket to Brisvegas. Surely you didn't think I was going to head overseas to the real 'Sin City' Las Vegas. While that would have been fantastic, the idea of being locked up in a cell with 20 men in a Las Vegas watchhouse didn't really appeal to me. It would've been fun, with a double order of trouble if I actually could've managed to organise that trip to the desert.

But no, I was to stay on Terra Australis, and jet up north to Brisbane. Why Brisbane? I am not sure. It was to be a landing point; I think my plan was to hitchhike down the coast to my friend's property in Dorrigo. Well, that was the loose plan anyway. I had no real agenda, I just needed to get out of town for some reason. I think that the main reason was I just could not sit still. I was elevated. When manic, most bipolar people tend to make snap decisions, usually bad ones leaving the finer points out of the equation.

I do enjoy the freedom of no fixed agenda and sometimes it just feels good to fly by the seat of my pants. In this case I decided to take Qantas flight QF563 to Brisbane and yes, I do recall my intention was to make it down to Dorrigo to spend some time with The Govna.

I had a wonderful flight and landed in Brisbane around 9 pm. I didn't have much money so decided that I would walk to the city. I only had my backpack, so I was travelling light. As I exited the terminal, I saw a sign that showed me the direction towards the city. I started my walk in that direction thinking it can't be that far. I didn't see any signs with a distance marker saying *"X kilometres to the city"*, I just kept walking and walking further away from the terminal. I ended up hitting the two-lane highway. I must have walked about 35 minutes at this point and the terminal lights started to look distant. The road ahead of me was not that brightly lit, and I continued. I was about an hour into my walk and there was still no sign of the city, I felt as if I was on a highway to nowhere.

It was getting cold, and I started to think that this was a terrible idea. I could see that the city lights in the distance were a long way off. I thought, *holy crap, I don't see any taxis coming, and I have limited money, so I'm in a bit of a pickle.*

I decided I was going to hitchhike. But there was only one thing missing, and that was a stream of traffic that might be able to give me a ride. It was a bleak situation, and the orange glow of streetlights provided no guiding light or comfort. I was seriously a long way out of town.

My first few attempts at pulling a car over failed. I was getting despondent. Then about 40 minutes later a guy in a ute pulled over and asked me where I was going. I told him to Brisbane city. He told me I was in luck, and he could give me a ride. I was so thankful, and hopped in. He told me he was driving back from Redcliffe where he was visiting his mother. I thanked him, and he said, 'No worries.'

He then said, 'You realise you're about 20 kilometres from town?' I didn't realise. 'But don't worry I will give you a ride to wherever you want to go.'

What a great man, were all Queenslanders this friendly? I was about to find out. My new friend dropped me off in the city, and I thanked him, and I went about trying to find a hotel that was going to be friendly. By friendly I mean a hotel that was happy to accept my story and give me a night of accommodation with no deposit, or credit card down. I did mention to you that I hardly had any money, certainly not enough to pay $170 for a hotel room.

I found a hotel on my first attempt and told them that I had lost my wallet, however I was an executive working for a gold mining company and my boss would be more than happy, correction, my boss would gladly pay for two- or three–nights' accommodation first thing in the morning. The night desk manager looked me up and down and asked which company I was working for. I told him, and reassured him that there was not a problem, and that the money for the room would be paid by 10 am.

I must have been convincing as I got a room. I could not believe my luck. I went upstairs and it was a relief to be in a safe environment. I unpacked a few items, took a warm shower, turned on the TV and jumped into bed. In the morning I rang my boss Abe, and he was surprised that I was in Brisbane.

'What are you doing there?' He asked.

I told him I had to check a few things out, but I plan on being back in a few days.

Abe was a man of faith, but I think he might have been losing a bit of faith in me at this stage. He paid the deposit and two nights' accommodation. He said,

'Please don't forget to bring me the receipt, and then you will be able to pay back your bill on your return, to our company.

'I understand, and thank you for doing this,' I said to Abe, 'Also, would you be able to advance me three hundred dollars from this month's pay?'

I was about to get my salary on the following Friday, but I was running on fumes.

He said, 'Moishe, this time only. Please manage your funds.'

Abe was a kind man, but this was pushing the boundaries of my employment. I feel as if he had almost adopted a naughty son.

With my hotel room booked for two nights I could relax. I had money coming into my account so I could get some food. I ordered some room service and spent most of the day in my room. I did take my medication with me and while I was manic, I had enough sense to take those pills, maybe not a therapeutic dose, but enough of a dose to calm down a bit.

It was about 4 pm and I decided to go for a walk. I walked out of the hotel and headed to the mall in the centre of town. It was a short walk to get there and once there, I had a good look around the shops and enjoyed the people watching as I made my way from one end of the shopping mall to the other. I think it took me about 30 minutes to get to the end of the mall, and I decided to grab myself a cup of coffee. I sat down at one of the last coffee shops that were still open and ordered myself a triple shot espresso.

I still had not worked out why I was so impulsive and why of all places I ended up in Brisbane. The one thing I knew was that I had to leave town. I just felt that I was going to end up in trouble if I stayed in Bondi, and I wanted to avoid the laughing academy and the four weeks of vacation that they would schedule for me if I got caught. I was taking my meds that I had with me, and they were making me sleepy. Taking the right dose was always tricky. I was certainly not thinking strange manic thoughts. By that I mean there was nothing supernatural or unnatural in my thinking.

I had been in good mental health and landed this dream job working for Abe. I had my wits about me. I could not afford to stuff up this amazing work opportunity. I was aware the mania had crept in and I needed some time-out to wind down before I had to be restrained with a few weeks in the cooler. I took my meds, but maybe not enough. It is always such a hard balancing act and I think I added too many balls to this juggling routine. Nonetheless, I kept the balls moving in the air, and I was out of Bondi where my chances of capture were a lot higher.

Over the past few years, I have learnt to accept and respect the fact that I have bipolar disorder type one, and it wasn't going away, my thinking was always being evaluated with a huge magnifying glass. It had to be, along with my behaviour.

As I sat there in the mall watching the people walk by, my thoughts were deep as I kept looking for answers as to why I ran away from Sydney. I had a great job, and I was being well paid, and knew my boss Abe was not fussed where I was so long as I was safe. He knew my work wasn't taking me to Brisbane, it was just me and my impulsive desire to flee Bondi and Sydney town and that troubled me.

CHAPTER 34
Holy Smokes!

I finished my coffee but was now craving a cigarette, it was one of the items I wanted to grab on my walk. I bought a pack and lit one up as I walked along. I was not a regular smoker but when I was elevated, I did enjoy a cigarette. As I drew in the tobacco, I had a mini epiphany and it dawned on me as to why I flew to Brisbane. My idea was to land there and head down the coast to go and stay with a friend of mine, The Govna, who had this offgrid bolthole high above the Bellingen Valley in the mountaintop town of Dorrigo in NSW.

Usually, I would get in a car and drive up to Dorrigo, the trip would normally take about seven hours. This time I thought it was going to be faster if I fly to Brisbane and drive to Dorrigo. I was still clearly elevated, and while sensible enough to ensure I was to keep my faculties from double and triple and quadruple checking every idea that was esoteric or not of this earth, the manic feeling while being suppressed to some degree with the meds I was taking, still had me motoring at twice the speed a brain should be revving at. At least I managed to get some sleep the night before, that was great, but now I had to work out how I was going to get to The Govna's bolthole. I knew I was going to be safe there and away from any aggravation.

The sun was now starting to set, and I was walking myself back to the hotel. I was not far off, and I could see the hotel at the end of the mall, maybe 250 metres away. The sun was really starting to disappear now and what I thought I was seeing was confirmed. I saw the lights of three fire trucks outside the hotel I was staying in.

I looked at the upper floors of the hotel and I could see that there was some commotion on the 4th floor of the hotel. It then dawned on me that I was staying on the 4th floor of the hotel. I picked up my pace and got to the hotel. There were people all over the street, and the lobby was full as well. I went to the counter and asked what was going on and they said, 'There was a fire. It was started in your room.'

I said, 'That's impossible.'

They said, 'We believe it was started with a cigarette.' I knew now that it could not have been me because I left the room in search of buying a pack.

I asked them for another room, the manager looked at me, and said, 'You have got to be kidding. You have destroyed three rooms.'

I told him that it could not have been me. I was out and didn't have cigarettes. I told him it must have been an electrical fault.

'Electrical fault?' He said, bewildered.

I said, 'Yes, I didn't have any cigarettes. Now, can I please have another room?'

In the packed lobby with guests that were all evacuated from their rooms on a Monday night, the manager looked at me with daggers in his eyes and said, 'No, get the F out of here!'

I said, 'Well actually no, I need somewhere to stay the night.'

He said, 'Here's your backpack,' which he then threw at me, 'NOW GET OUT! F OFF!' The look on his face was quite serious. The fire brigade was already there in numbers, and I certainly didn't want him to call the cops on me. It was dark outside now and the lights of the fire trucks were flashing all around the lobby of the hotel. I could feel his intent, and he really needed to blame someone for all this ruckus, and allegedly the fire did start in my room, to this day I still stand by the cause of the fire being an electrical fault. I was not going to accept responsibility for upsetting all of these lovely house guests' time in Brisvegas.

I held my soaking backpack and was contemplating where I was going to go. I just could not push my luck at this place any longer; it was time to go. By now I was also ravenous, and I wanted to ask the manager for a free meal in the bistro before leaving. After all, room service was off the cards. I felt like I was really being inconvenienced by this fire as much as any of the other guests.

I mean for all I know they may have just wanted to do some room refurbishments on the 4th floor in room 401 and saw me coming! Blame it on the manic Jewish guy. The bats were flying around my stomach at a furious pace now, and the scene was rather chaotic. I think every guest had now been evacuated from their rooms and was either pushing their way around in the crowded lobby or spilt out onto the street. It was a scene for sure.

I liked the idea of having one of their delightful club sandwiches, but with all the chaos I think I might have found it difficult to swallow and keep my dinner down. I glanced over at the manager who was now attending to a line of people at the front desk. He glanced over to me and asked, 'Why are you still here? I asked you to leave!'

No problem, sir! Screw the club sandwich, and with that I made my way through the crowd of people who were inconvenienced. I wanted to apologise to them, but that may mean admitting guilt to this whole kerfuffle, and there is no way I caused all of this. I just could not accept that kind of responsibility. No. I am convinced it was an electrical fire and that is that. It may have started in my room, but that was purely happenstance. I wasn't even there!

I had enough of doing this post-mortem and thought to myself that I had bigger issues to worry about. A hungry belly and a roof over my head for the night for starters. My backpack was totally soaked and let me just say Brisbane does get cold in winter and now it was dark, and the temperature had dropped considerably to about 13 degrees Celsius; I had to find a place to stay for the night. I was really beginning to the think that this cut and run trip was a terrible idea, but at least I had my freedom. Was I paranoid about the Bondi Police? Of course I was. I had been on their radar before, and they knew me well. I was one phone call away from another unpaid holiday at the puzzle factory, I had to leave town.

I was also convinced that I was able to look after my manic brain on my own so I had to prove to myself that I could be responsible and bring this minor elevation down in my own way. After all, I had accepted my condition which was a huge thing, and I also had the weapons of mass destruction. Mood stabilisers and antipsychotics, a whole pharmacopoeia of meds to wind down this elevation. I just needed a safe place to do so. Obviously, Brisbane was not the safe environment that I thought it was.

I was so glad that my backpack was not consumed in the fire! This was another reason why I thought this so-called fire seemed so convenient. How on earth could they get to my room that quickly to save my backpack, yet the room was destroyed by the flames? This was indeed a mystery that I would've loved to have worked out, but I doubt they would have let me into the scene of the crime. Best to let it go for now. If I pushed it any harder, that manager would have called the cops for sure.

I wandered around the city for about 45 minutes and found a hostel. I had some money wired to me earlier that day by Abe, enough to get me through to payday, so I was now able to pay for the room. The night manager of the hostel looked at me and asked how he could help. I said I would like a single room please. He said he had one room left. Or I could have a shared room. I said, 'No, I will take the single room.'

'$69,' he replied.

'Great.' I gave him my card. I thought how lucky I was that I had my intact wallet with me, it might have easily ended up soaked or destroyed in the inferno.

The night manager then asked, 'Is your backpack wet?'

I said, 'Yes'.

He asked what happened, 'Did it end up in the river?' I said to him, 'If I told

you, you probably would not believe me.'

'Really?' He asked.

I said, 'It's a long story and not worth going into. Can I please have the key to my room?'

At this point I thought that the soaked backpack was some kind of sign to him that all was not right in wonderland, but he looked at me and asked, 'Are you planning on staying a few days?'

I said, 'I am not sure at this stage, can I let you know in the morning?'

He said, 'Sure, I just need to know if I have to hold the room for you.'

I said, 'I'm exhausted and hungry. Can I please tell you first thing in the morning exactly how many days I plan on staying? In fact, I will definitely be staying tomorrow night. I will pay for that in the morning.'

That was fine by him. I asked if there was anything open and he told me, 'I'm afraid you're out of luck. Nothing opens 'till about 7 am.' So much for the bright lights of Brisvegas!

You could have fired a shotgun down the main street and not hit a soul. I was glad to be off the streets, and I began to unpack my soaked belongings. My room was far from lux, but it was cosy with a double bed and heater. The room was warm in minutes, and just as well because I needed to dry my stuff. I placed my belongings all around the room and I thought how lucky I was not to have lost all my possessions in the blaze.

I cranked the heater in the room up to ten. The whole drama of the hotel wiped me out, and I decided to take a double dose of my 'calm me down' antipsychotic meds, put the mindless TV onto some drone rubbish channel with some crappy show on for background noise, then I lay on the bed totally exhausted. I pulled my beanie over my eyes and blacked out.

I stayed in that room for an extra two nights until my belongings dried out, and on the third day I decided to give The Govna a call to ask if it was okay to make my way down the coast to his off-grid mountain-top retreat. He said, 'Of course, come on over.'

I then asked, 'Can you pick me up from Coffs Harbour?' I knew that I was pushing the friendship, but he was fine with that. I packed my backpack, thanked the day manager, and asked him for directions to the right bus terminal. He told me it was only about a 25-minute walk, and he drew a little map for me. I was thrilled to be on my way out of Brisbane.

The manager of the hostel gave fantastic directions; they were spot on. I found the Greyhound Coach Service bus terminal and made it to the ticket counter. The ticket vendor said I was lucky as the next bus was sold out; however, he did have one seat available on the 1 pm service from a cancellation. I told him it must be my lucky day; 'Can I please buy that?' The ticket vendor said, 'Of course,' and I pulled my card out. With one tap of the card, I now had the last ticket away from the bright and boring lights of Brisbane. What can I say, except that drama and trouble seemed to follow me no matter where I went. I thanked the ticket vendor, and he gave me my receipt and asked me to be there before the departure time.

I told him that I would not be late for this bus ride to happy land, and I also thought I might as well buy a lottery ticket as my luck must be changing! Hopefully the bus won't run out of gas or drive off a cliff. I wanted to ring my boss Abe just to let him know that all was okay, but I thought he would still be in *shul*, it was just past 9 am. Instead, I rang Mike and told him all was well, and I was going to visit an old friend somewhere off-the-grid outside of the mountain-top town of Dorrigo.

Mike asked if all was okay and I said, 'Yes.' He asked if I was taking my medication and I told him that I was. He sounded relieved, 'Please don't slip up, and make sure you're taking your meds.'

I said, 'Mate, of course, I would not risk forgetting. Who knows what might happen.' I asked him if he had any new projects to look at and he told me there was one, but he was taking care of it. He said, 'You just look after yourself. Did you really need to get out of town? I was a bit surprised at how quickly you disappeared.'

I said, 'When you gotta go, you gotta go!'

I reassured Mike and told him I would be fine, 'I think a week or so in the treetop off-grid forests of *Rambatan* with The Govna are going to do me the world of good.'

Mike agreed, 'Take care and call me in a few days.'

'For sure.' I then rang The Govna and told him that I would be arriving in Coffs Harbour no later than 6 pm. He was not thrilled but agreed to pick me up.

CHAPTER 35
On The Road To Rambatan

I bought some snacks for the five and a half-hour bus ride to Coffs Harbour and hopped aboard the bus for the ride down the coast. The trip seemed to go fairly quickly, and we finally arrived in Coffs Harbour just before 6 pm. I couldn't wait to see The Govna and as we pulled into the terminus, I could see him sitting inside his trusty diesel 4WD idling across the road from the bus stop. I grabbed my bag, thanked the driver, and walked across the road to jump into The Govna's 4WD.

The Govna and I go way back. We were business associates in the lifestyle business back in the early '90s. Now you may be wondering what the lifestyle business is. Well, it's the sale of organic vegetables for combustion. Okay, I will cut to the chase and say we both sold weed. Me to him, and him to his eclectic and boutique clientele. The Govna was always a wildlife warrior way before Steve Irwin became famous with that term, and he taught me a lot about nature and giving back in the form of reforestation. This was something that he was passionate about. Oh, and yes, he had no problem handling snakes, something I was just not fond of. As for wrestling and relocating crocs, that was not his thing.

I was introduced to him by a Russian mafia crime figure, or so he thought he was, whose name was Vladimir. Vlad didn't want to do the legwork and decided to introduce me to The Govna while still charging a hefty fee for doing diddly squat. Back in the early '90s, The Govna had a boutique retail weed dispensary located in the premier suburb of Point Piper and he ran very tight hours for the shop which was known as The Cave.

Business hours were between 4 pm and 7.30 pm. Bad luck if you wanted to score after those hours. The Govna, while being very open in his thinking could have branched out into other party favourites such as cocaine or ecstasy, but he refrained from doing so as he was not into selling Class A drugs. There were plenty of others such as Vladimir who were happy to look after people who did desire these drugs, but not The Govna. He was a man of strong values and was not motivated by greed. Of course, he could have made a fortune selling these drugs but power to him, if it was not plant-based, then he was not interested.

The Govna did offer his clients a variety of pot both natural and hydroponic as well as hash. Hashish was available in the '90s. There was brown hard hash and the soft black putty which was much stronger. The chronic hydroponic indoor weed seemed to be very popular and in no time The Govna and I were doing some good business, or as I like to call it, community service.

Over time, The Govna and I became very good friends. He enjoyed my sense of humour, and I loved his wisdom. He began opening up to me about his past. The Govna told me his father served in the British military in a very high-ranking position. During the late '50s and '60s, his father was appointed to be the caretaker of Borneo at the behest of the Queen of the United Kingdom; his posting was a very serious role. The Govna Senior had the highest post that the United Kingdom could bestow upon a man when being a caretaker in a foreign land. I can't say for sure what his title was, but I did see some pictures of the young Govna and his family life from those times and they were treated like royalty. The young Govna was raised with lots of help in their royal home of Borneo, so he was a tad spoilt to say the least. I think even during breakfast the young Govna had the royal milk carefully poured for him on his royal cornflakes every morning, and with that kind of upbringing it was amazing that he could be so down-to-earth. Was he spoilt? Of course he was, but he loved being raised like a royal.

Meanwhile, business was going well between us and like most businesses in the free world, I gave him credit to ensure he always had plenty of stock on hand. This was going to be the source of some pain later, but I was amazed when I would frequent The Cave between opening hours to watch the eclectic procession of people that came through his shop, it was something to be witnessed. Vladimir meanwhile was getting a clip for every ounce of weed that was being sold. This was nothing short of *chutzpah*. He was doing no work and taking no risk, but that's the kind of guy he was.

Eventually, The Govna complained to me that this arrangement was ridiculous, and I suggested we stop paying him, seeing that he wasn't doing any of the work anyway. So that's what we did. In hindsight, I should have given him a grand or two, at the time just to keep him off my case, but we decided he had made enough free money.

As our friendship grew, The Govna told me about his property in Dorrigo and invited me to come up and stay. I could hardly wait to get there as I had seen some photos, but they didn't do the place justice. When I got to the property, I was totally captivated by the amazing natural beauty that surrounded the property. He told me I was welcome to visit the place and stay for as long as I liked. As a budding horticulturalist and lover of all things nature, I was very keen to go and visit this place to see and experience it first-hand. The invitation was open and I could come anytime whether he was there or not.

I gave the mountain-top home the name of *Rambatan*. It seemed appropriate. The drive back from Coffs Harbour took about an hour. We climbed the Dorrigo Mountain view road, which was a steep two-lane winding road, we then took a left onto a country road which finally led us to the gate at the top paddock. This was the start of the property, and it was about a 1 kilometre drive through this paddock, carefully staying on the track as the grass was high and mudsoaked from the high rainfall. Once through the paddock, there was a final mud-soaked, almost vertical hill that was no easy feat to drive up. If you walked up, you might end up doing so on hands and knees, it was so steep and slippery, and that was when it was not raining. Dorrigo is 800 metres above sea level, and it had a very high rainfall. To drive up this final steep hill, you really needed to have some good driving skills. This hill could not be tackled by a normal car, and even if you had a 4WD you also needed to be an experienced off-road driver to get up this heartbreak hill. Many people got caught thinking they had the skills to get up this 200 metre track, only to be caught somewhere in the middle, bogged down. Once up this final pass, you were in an off-grid rainforest paradise.

The house was a handmade unique home that looked like something right out of the pages of *The Hobbit* or *The Lord of the Rings*. The house was hand-built from materials sourced locally. The home even had a towering tarot spire on the right of the house. It really looked like something from *Middleearth*. It really was straight out of a fairytale. It was powered by hydroelectricity generated from the waterfall that ran down one side of the property. A small turbine was placed in the fastflowing section of the moving water, and this was connected to the longest power cord I had ever seen. This power cord ran up to the house and was connected to some kind of converter which in turn converted the energy into 12V electricity. There were also some batteries to store this power, but this had its limitations. Appliances such as a toaster were not allowed to be used as they were too much of a drain on the system. The fridge was always on, but that ran on 12V, and there was enough power left over for computers and the luxury of TV and DVD's. Luckily, we could use the vacuum cleaner for short bursts. Dinner was cooked on an original wood-fired stove cooker. It was just like the old days, just with some minimal luxuries.

The wood stove had enough room on top of it for four pots or pans. If you were planning on cooking a meal you had to plan well ahead. This meant collecting the wood, starting the fire, then you had to work it like any fire till it had a good flame going. From there it was easy as you just needed to top up the fire with some more wood to keep the hotplates going. In winter this also doubled as a second fireplace. It was pleasant in that galley-style kitchen and I loved the whole process of making dinner there.

The Govna ran a very open-door policy for those he invited to his mountain-top retreat. Some guests even stayed for months on end, while others would pop in for a few days to break up their road trip. When I went there the first time there was a man who was an artist who would collect items such as animal bones from the surrounding area and make art from them. He also drew with black ink on white butcher's paper. He was an incredibly talented person who enjoyed living there full-time as a caretaker of the place when The Govna was not in residence. The truth was that someone had to live there to keep the house going. It was a living organism that needed humans to keep it alive. A magical house in a special spiritual place, perched on the precipice of the Dorrigo Mountain.

The view from the loungeroom was nothing short of spectacular. We could sit in an assortment of well-worn furniture, and just stare out of the huge glass sliding doors, peering into the Bellingen Valley below us. There were huge mountain ridges either side of the valley and you could never get sick of such natural beauty. On certain days, after heavy rain, the mist would be thick. Especially after heavy rain, this thick mist looked like clouds beneath you with clear skies above, as if flying on a plane. It really felt as if you were in the heavens looking down on the earth below.

The toilet, which was away from the house, was called *The Thunderbox*. It was a natural latrine with 15 stairs taking you up to this private bog hut, which had a commanding view of the Bellingen Valley below.

To this day I have never sat on a toilet that had a view to match this throne. I know that some people love to sit on the can and read or spend hours on the dunny. I have never been one of these people, but being on this throne, was an exception. You could sit here and just take in the majestic view while lightening your load. Where the latrine ended, I have no idea, but I am sure that was taken care of by nature. It was primal but a fantastic dumping box.

Most winter nights were spent in the loungeroom which had a huge fireplace and a fire raging away inside. It was peaceful, you could lay back in a beanbag with a good book or just drift away in thought as you gazed blankly at the open fire.

CHAPTER 36
Who's Your Mate?

I was surprised when we got to the house that there was no one else around. I loved this as I could just hang out with The Govna one-on-one. Two days rolled by, and the rain had set in hard. I am talking horizontal rain. It was a brutal storm pattern that was not going to relent for a few more days. We had enough food to get by so there was no urgency to get food supplies in town. The outside temperature was also a chilly 4 degrees Celsius at night. It was snowing in the town of Armidale which was only about an hour away along the plateau. But no snow here. We rugged up with the warm clothing that we had and did our best to keep the wood dry.

It was my third day in paradise; I had enjoyed the tranquil atmosphere and read a great book for most of the time. I still had some mania in me, but also had meds to take the edge off.

Day turned into night, and we made a tasty but simple scrambled egg and veg dish, pumped up the volume on the fire, and began relaxing in the upstairs private study where the small TV, DVD player, and library were. It was a cosy space with a wrap-around lounge to lay back on, a very comfortable space for movie watching. As we were deciding on which DVD to watch, there was a loud knock on the door downstairs. We both looked at each other, wondering who on earth was there. We were not expecting anyone, and it was almost 8 pm. We came down the stairs to find an estranged friend of The Govna's standing inside the entrance way. We could not believe what we saw.

The gentlemen was a man named Arthur, who had come unannounced. He was soaked to the skin and barefoot, with a bit of a wild look in his eyes.

The Govna said, 'Don't worry, I know him,' but even he was a bit surprised. How on earth did he make it up the rocky mud hill to the house, barefoot?

Arthur looked at us and said, 'I walked.'

'Really? But it's raining and freezing outside, and you're barefoot.'

Arthur said, 'I know but I'm fine. I walked in from town.'

We gave him a towel and some dry clothes to change into. There was something not right about this visitor.

'Would you like a hot tea?' I asked him.

'Yes please,' he replied. While I made him a cup of tea, The Govna who knew Arthur had some mental health issues in the past, namely schizophrenia, decided to call his family.

They told The Govna that Arthur was in a psych ward in Sydney, and he did not return that day from lunch. He obviously had enough money for a bus ticket to Dorrigo and absconded with no personal items or even shoes. How he managed to walk all the way from town to the property which was 7 kilometres away in the dark was one thing, but to get through the paddock and up the final hill barefoot was beyond comprehension. His feet must have been cut to pieces.

We asked him a few questions, but he was a bit evasive. The Govna was asked by his family to keep him there overnight and the following day. His father would drive up and collect him from town. We fed Arthur, and then he took a shower. We then showed him where he was going to sleep for the night. I asked him if he would like to join us for the movie, but he declined. He then asked if he could look around the shed.

The shed had an open-plan bedroom above it. That was where I was sleeping when I didn't fall asleep in front of the fire. This large room also had a combustion log fireplace, and I loved the space. I wasn't sure if I felt completely safe there, after all our new house guest was not playing with a full deck. But then again, who was I to judge? I was still a tad manic myself, and I had met people like Arthur before, so I wasn't all that worried.

The Govna said that it was fine for him to go to the shed and have a sticky beak. He reassured me that Arthur was harmless, and I had nothing to worry about. We, on the other hand, settled in to watch a movie. We finished watching the movie and then it dawned on us that Arthur had been rather quiet. We had to see where he was and what he was doing.

He was not downstairs passed out in front of the fire as we first thought, so we ran out into the rain and found him in the shed. We could not believe our eyes when we walked into the shed. Arthur had pulled The Govna's motorbike to pieces. It was all on the wooden sleepers; the bike had been turned into parts.

The Govna was not impressed, and simply said, 'Arthur, what have you done? Can you please put the bike back together again, now?'

He said, 'Sure,' he was just amusing himself. We thought that this was going to be beyond him, and we felt it best to sit with him for a while. Bit by bit we watched him as he assembled the motorbike back together. This was totally nuts; it is always harder to put things back together, no matter if it is a jigsaw puzzle or a motorbike. Two hours had passed but he did it. He actually put the bike back into one piece. It was nothing short of crazy. Or maybe that was just the way he turned up!

By this time, we were all tired. We knew we had to keep Arthur in our company during the following day until his family arrived in town later in the afternoon to take him back home. Maybe tomorrow we could find another motorbike for him to take apart or a small tractor possibly. Sadly, there was no such machinery around, instead we asked if he felt like crashing out. He seemed exhausted after his journey and mechanical exercises.

We showed him to a comfortable place to lay down and then The Govna and I both retired to our beds. The following day, the rain had eased. We ate breakfast, and then went for a walk down the steep embankment along the river, which had turned into a raging torrent from all the rain.

Walking around that high rainforest, it was important to have good clothing on. Especially high socks around the ankles as the leeches were everywhere looking for a good meal. They're an ugly little bloodsucker should one attach itself to you, and sometimes no matter how well you prepare, you might find one on your ankle, or foot.

We built a fire in the loungeroom to keep warm, we read, made cups of tea, and shared war stories. We were trying to find out how Arthur made it up to the house in the dark and pouring rain without a flashlight. It was still beyond our comprehension. He remained very elusive, just saying that he had been here a few times before, so he knew his way around.

The day rolled by and The Govna received a call from Arthur's father who said he was close by, so we headed into town to do some shopping and waited with Arthur to meet his father. We had been in town about an hour and were waiting in a café when Arthur's dad walked in. He saw us with Arthur and was relieved. I don't think that Arthur was all that happy to see his dad, but we were glad to hand him over. His father thanked us for looking after him and told us that he did in fact abscond from a locked ward. He was indeed a real magician!

Now he was in the safety and care of his father, and on his way back to Sydney for part two of his time back in a laughing academy.

The Govna and I still reminisce about this story, it never gets old, and will always remain some kind of mystery, the mystery of Arthur.

CHAPTER 37
Two Weeks Respite

A week had rolled by, and I was beginning to get anxious. I had to get back to Sydney. I asked The Govna if he could take me to Coffs Harbour where I could catch a plane back home.

He said, 'No problem. Find out what time you need to go, and I will take you.'

I checked the flights and there was one leaving at 1 pm the following day. I felt extremely agitated and was short on meds as well, so I could not bring the horrible feeling under control. My thinking was starting to go a little off. My mind began racing.

It was nighttime now and I was in the studio above the shed. Suddenly, I started fuelling the wood stove, and as I loaded the wood in, I started having horrific thoughts about the Holocaust. I just could not get these thoughts out of my head about what my family went through. As I placed the wood in the fire, I started to name them after Nazi war criminals like I was performing some kind of ritual. Placing the wood in, I would say their names, one at a time, followed by, 'Burn you bastards! Burn in hell! Himmler here's a log for you, you bastard!'

I opened the glass door, put the wood inside. It burned away and I danced around the room in a trance like state as I watched the log burn. As it burnt down, I opened the glass door again.

'Göring this log's for you. May you burn in hell like this log I prepared just for you!'

'Mengele, here is one I especially prepared for you.'

I wanted this log to burn long and slow. I placed it into the furnace. I then I continued to do my tribal dance around the room, and watched the logs burn away. I was getting carried away.

It was extremely emotional, but in some way, it was cathartic. I was getting myself worked up for sure. I moved on to Hitler now, I was deep in this ritual, but I ran out of wood. So, I decided to put my mobile phone in the furnace.

'Burn, Adolf, burn! May your soul burn in hell!'

I don't know why I did that, but I did. I was really elevated for sure, but I was swept away in the whole ceremony of the situation. I had to admit that it also felt so good to think that my paganistic ritual was helping to add fire to their souls burning in hell.

Now this was not some Jewish revenge ceremony, it was my own PTSD coming to the surface and being played out. Did it make me feel better? You bet it did.

I watched as my phone popped and crackled in the flames, not thinking about the ramifications of not having a phone. That didn't matter to me. I needed to inflict the pain by fire on these war criminals and looking back, the whole scene was bonkers, but I was motoring with an elevated head, and I was releasing some anger for the loss of my family, and all of those that perished during that horrible time.

As the flames devoured my phone, I hoped that the soul of that man who caused so much death and destruction on the world would feel every lick from every flame. I got so swept up in this ceremony, and it went on for hours. By the time the fire started to die down I was exhausted. I lay on the bed and passed out. I had never done anything like that before. I certainly didn't plan it out, it just came over me and it seemed like a good idea. As for my phone? Well, I was going to need another one, but I could wait until I got back to Sydney to buy it.

In the morning, I rang Abe using The Govna's phone and told him I was coming back to Sydney. I booked a flight, packed my stuff and got ready for the drive down the mountain to the airport.

We arrived at the airport, and I bid The Govna farewell, and thanked him for his hospitality. It was enjoyable spending the last few days away, but I was antsy inside. 'See you next time my friend!' The Govna said, 'Have a safe flight and please look after yourself.' I am sure The Govna was happy to have me but also happy to see me head back to Sydney.

With that I jumped out of the 4WD and headed into the terminal. Once I was in the terminal at the airport, I was totally on edge. I went to the ticketing counter and picked up my ticket for the flight. I was given the ticket for seat A1. Of course, the number meant something to me, but I thought it just seemed appropriate. I wasn't going to read too much into the numerology. Call me paranoid, but I felt as if people began looking at me in a strange way, and I didn't like it. I was pacing about, and it was not a large airport to say the least.

But I was manic, and instead of being friendly and greeting them with a smile, I was nasty.

If they looked me in the eyes without saying anything, just staring at me, I would say, 'What are you looking at?'

This kept happening over and over, with different people, and I didn't feel at ease. More people walked by and stared me in the eyes, and I would say, 'What the 'F' are you looking at?'

I was being aggressive, but for some reason, even more people just looked at me as if I had two heads or was on fire. This seemed to go on for about 20 minutes, and I obviously upset a few of my fellow travellers whose glaring looks were giving me the shits. I don't know why I was that irritated by this, but I was. I should not have lashed out, I should have calmed my angry head, but no. Then just when I least expected it, I was slammed to the ground from behind by four cops. It was a cheap shot as they really could have approached me from the front and we could have had a brief chat and I would have said my apologies to the fellow travellers, and that would have been that. But no, they got me on the deck, picked me up and escorted me into the back of a paddy wagon.

I sat in the mobile cage like a trapped animal. I had no idea what the cops were going to do with me or where they were going to take me, but when they came into sight, I gave them an earful, calling them a host of colourful names and commending them on their excellent police work. I was lucky that they didn't throw the cuffs on me, spray me with the mace, or even taser me. I was outnumbered, and as usual, seemed to have enough common sense to know when the jig was up. As for where they were going to take me, well, that was about to be revealed.

Twenty minutes later, two cops got in the mobile prison, and we started to drive somewhere. I didn't have an in-depth knowledge of the area so where I was going was a mystery. I could safely say it was not to some private jet or luxury resort. The drive was about 15 minutes or so and we pulled up at the front of the Coffs Harbour psych hospital. One of the police hopped out, came to the back of the van, and asked me if I was going to cause any problems. I said, 'No'.

The cop then told me if I caused any problems, he would do whatever he had to, 'So be on your best behaviour.'

Again, I said to him, 'I am not going to give him any issues,' and with that, he opened the back door of the wagon to let me out. I was escorted into the puzzle factory and could not believe I had been red-carded again. My behaviour was off, and yes, I was being passive aggressive, or maybe just aggressive, but either way, my plans to head back to Sydney were now going to be messed up. For how long? Well, that was going to be up to me.

I sat in the admissions area waiting for the doctors and eventually they came out. They asked me a whole series of questions, and I admitted to them that I was a bit elevated. The Admissions Doctor said to me that they were going to keep me in the locked ward for an undisclosed period. I asked if it was going to be days or weeks. He told me that depended on me and how quickly I responded to treatment. But he did say that it was going to be a minimum of two weeks. I was annoyed, but in no position to argue the ruling. I asked if I could make a phone call or two to let my family know. The doctor said, 'Of course, let's just finish your admission and then you can ring whoever you like.'

The doctor finished his welcome routine and one of the nurses came around to ask me if I would like a sandwich and a cup of something to drink. I said, 'Thank you, that would be lovely,' and I asked if I could make two calls.

She said, 'Of course, follow me.'

I was taken into an office, and I grabbed the phone and rang Mike. When he answered I told him not to be concerned, and that I would not be coming back to Sydney today. I am in the laughing academy at Coffs Harbour and will be out in two weeks. I let him know that I was acting out at the airport and for my crime, managed to find my way into this place to cool my heels. 'How do you know you're going to get out in two weeks?'

'Call it a lucky guess.' Normally, it's a four-week vacation but I was being optimistic.

After that call, I rang my mother and told her that I was going to stay up here for another few weeks. I told her I was having a great break but needed some more time away. I just didn't want her to worry, and besides, there was nothing that she could do except mail me a cake, no file in it, just the cake.

My time in this small institution was boring as usual, but the days seemed to roll on by. There was a decent amount of time spent finger painting and watching boring TV to help pass my time away. The food seemed to be the usual hospital food which made me wonder if they had the same chef as the Sydney psych ward. I suppose it was better than no food at all.

One day I saw this huge biker looking character get himself all worked up. The orderlies came running in from all directions and he cleaned up the first two with some handy punches to the head. The next three overpowered him and managed to get him on the ground where he was quickly sedated with the dart of a thousand slumbers. More orderlies came in and together they picked him up and dragged him off to some private locked room to sleep off his bad attitude. Maybe he didn't like the food on the menu either, or maybe he was sick of being locked up against his will.

Either way, it was interesting to watch, and the lesson I took away was to never argue with the staff. If they could bring down a big man like him, I had no chance. I complied to all that was asked of me every day, and two weeks rolled by. The senior psych doctor came to my room and told me that he was going to prepare my paperwork so I could leave. He went through a checklist of medications and said he would provide me with enough meds to last a week, but on arriving in Sydney I had to see my psych doctor, and that my doctor needed to send him a confirmation that I had indeed gone to the appointment. It was part of my bail conditions. I didn't have a problem with that.

While I told Mike I would be out in two weeks, I was just being optimistic. I had never been let out after two weeks before, so I was pleased when they told me that I could go without having to stay the usual four-weeks. Maybe they needed the bed, but I was certainly not going to ask for more time, I was ready to see the back of this place and my new friends. With my approval to leave in place, I asked if I could make a phone call or two and I rang Mike and asked him to plan for my flight back to Sydney the following day which he did. I also called my family to let them know I was coming back.

The following day I grabbed my bag and headed to the airport for my flight back. When I got to the terminal, I made sure that I had my happy friendly face on. Nothing like a couple of weeks in the puzzle factory to reset your attitude and bring me down to reality. Previoulsy I was acting out, agitated and being rude. I was manic and I did frighten my fellow travellers and there was no doubt I was being a public nuisance. The good news was I had no psychosis, or obsession with numerology, or any real stress to trigger the mania. My manic brain had deceived me, and I should have been aware of this so I could address the mood and bring things under control.

I think this is the hardest thing for me. Being able to read my mood at the start of this elevation was something that I had not mastered yet. With each mania and time in the locked wards I was getting better. The post-mortems in the Coffs Harbour psych ward allowed me to once again, look inside myself to learn what triggered the mania. I thought about it quite a lot, but I just could not work out when this elevation started. I think it was the night prior when I was doing my wood and phone sacrifice. I certainly never wanted to be locked up again that's for sure. I never wanted to get elevated either. I asked my Psych Dr if I was going to have elevations every year. He said, 'Unfortunately yes'.

He said that I just needed to be more self-aware, and then give him a call so he could adjust my medication accordingly. It was not great news, but I did start to become more aware when my brain began to speed up. Becoming self-aware and getting to know myself is the best thing I can do. As I wrote in previous chapters, mania in the beginning does feel good, a little too good. Having the motivation to avoid the puzzle factory was certainly a great reason to closely monitor my moods. Whilst I now accepted my condition, not living in denial was a huge step, but that was not the issue. I just love the energy that comes at the beginning of a mania. Most people with bipolar one do. As for why I got locked up, it was totally my fault, and I should not have been behaving the way I did.

Had I not acted out and been more self-aware that I was indeed manic, I could have just ignored everyone around me and sat patiently waiting for my flight. But no, I was being rude, and had no idea that my brain was spinning fast. Of course, there was that paganistic ritual I had in the studio. That should have been the first sign that things were off, but I will admit I did enjoy the ceremony and there was nobody there just me, the woodfired heater and the Lord. Looking back that was the start of the mania, I have no idea why that came over me, but it did feel good at the time doing my own form of voodoo!

I caught a cab to the airport for my flight and I was feeling good. I was over the moon that I only had to stay two weeks. That was a first for me. I was very happy to see the back of the Coffs Harbour and glad that my extended holiday in my home away from home had come to an end. Once again, the doctors had the elevation in my head ironed out. This time at the airport I was relaxed and on my best behaviour. With my new friendly attitude, I boarded the plane, sat back in my seat happy to say *'goodbye'* Coffs Harbour, and *'hello'* Sydney.

CHAPTER 38
Nothing Lasts Forever

I arrived back in Sydney and got back to working every day at the office. I'm not sure why, but I didn't have the usual severe depression that followed my manias. I was depressed but it wasn't the brutal, crippling depressions that I had experienced in the past. The ones that would keep me glued to my bed. The only thing I could put it down to was that this recent mania was nipped in the bud early, and while I did lose some face with Abe regarding the hotel room fire, I had a great job and I had to turn up each day for work. I also felt I had a responsibility to Abe to keep an eye on the companies we had made an investment into. I was being paid well for my effort, so I had to do the right thing.

The end of the year was approaching, and the hype and promise of the internet dot-com's started to turn for the worst. Investors were experiencing pain with these new IT companies that had so much potential on paper, but then it seemed like a game of musical chairs, and everyone was scrambling to find a seat and get their money back. Sadly, the hype of the dot-com boom started to implode all over the world. The companies with their crazy valuations hit a sobering reality. People who had invested in these companies that had not produced any revenue or profit began to lose faith and they started to pull their money out if they could. It was brutal for these early investors as dot-com turned to dot-bomb.

The market crashed. As for us, well we seemed to save most of our money from our projects, breaking even on one but losing money on the other. We certainly didn't make money, and the opportunity of hitting a winning product, began to slip away. In the end we decided to cut our losses, pulling out of the projects we were working on. I suppose that is the risk one takes in business. I'm sure if things didn't go south for the tech sector, we would've stuck it out and things might have turned out differently, but it wasn't to be.

Regarding my bipolar, I managed to find an understanding boss who was not judgemental. Even when my mania flared up and I was side-lined for two weeks, he welcomed me back to work, allowing me to get on with what I had to do for the company. It was a fun ride while it lasted. I certainly learnt a lot from Abe who was fantastic to work for. In total, I worked for Abe for about a year. I was no longer in denial, but sadly I still had a lot to learn, like knowing when the mania was creeping in and taking over my brain. I was lucky that the mania I had while working for Abe didn't hinder my position within the company. I was blessed to have the opportunity to work for him and I am fortunate to still have Abe as a good friend and mentor in my life. I had no idea what I was going to do next. I was so happy in my last work endeavour, but it was now time to find the next work adventure.

As usual it came with a few twists and turns.

CHAPTER 39
Let's Go Hunt Some Heads...

I was enjoying my time off, but I had to start looking for work, so I started searching through the salesperson wanted ads. I saw an ad from a recruitment company that was looking to hire a person with IT knowledge and sales skills to recruit IT people for the banking industry in Asia. I certainly had been to a few recruiters and thought I could do this line of work. I applied for the role, had two rounds of interviews, and beat 40 applicants to the job. Well, that is what they told me once I started.

I had no idea what it was going to be like, but the term boiler room would sum it up best. There were only ten of us in the company, and my desk was facing my manager. The other guys had their desks facing each other. If we were not on a call, it was easy to listen in on one of the other guy's phone calls to close sales, and in this company closing a sale meant we successfully placed a candidate in a new position. Our job was to find candidates for roles or find roles for candidates. We all had our vertical markets to focus on. The other guys in the company were recruiting candidates for roles in divisions such as stock traders, business analysts, fixed income or the mergers and acquisitions. I had no idea what those other divisions were about, but the salaries of these candidates were huge. The salaries for people working in IT positions in banks was much higher than a similar role outside of banking. If they worked for a bank, they could potentially earn anywhere from 30 to 40 percent more, or higher.

The banks wanted to hire the best IT people in their area of expertise. If any of the systems failed, the potential loss could easily run into the millions, so there was a lot of pressure to ensure all the technology (hardware and software) was running well. When the markets were good and the banks had a very profitable year, they would also reward their staff with additional bonuses. This was not guaranteed but when they were handing out bonuses, they were fantastic. If the markets were in decline the banks were brutal with cutting staff numbers. I remember one bank I worked with cut their IT department from 130 down to 15.

Of course, the bank would pay these people their redundancy, and in some cases that might be as much as a year's salary, but the bank didn't care. It was better for them to do this than have a department full of people with nothing to do.

Like any business, employee salaries would be the second largest expense, not knowing when things would turn around, it was more cost effective to retrench staff and build up their IT departments later when the market turned around. As soon as the markets did turn there were lots of roles, and finding good candidates became the issue.

When we made a placement, our company was not shy in charging the banks either. The company fee was 33-percent of the candidate's yearly salary. While the traders and other areas paid huge money, starting salaries for IT roles such as network engineers, or junior software developers varied from USD 150,000 to USD 200,000 per year, whereas the same role outside of banking might only pay USD 100,000 to USD 120,000 per year.

Some of the hiring managers (Heads of IT for a country) could be on USD 800,000 or more. That was the largest salary I had come across for a senior Head of Management position. While we were not set targets, I thought to myself that I only had to make five or six placements a year to make some good money.

The only other staff member working for the company was the secretary who did all the admin for us. She had a good sense of humour and I think she needed that to cope with all the macho chest-beating that went on between the guys. She was also rewarded with a small bonus when we would make a placement. Sometimes she needed to call candidates to confirm phone appointments or deal with the human resources department of the bank that was doing the hiring, and this was time consuming, so it was reasonable that she was rewarded financially as well when we had a win. She sat near the front of the office far enough away from us, so she wasn't a distraction or in earshot when the boss was dishing out the call to arms, in other words telling us to pick up the phone to make calls.

To be successful in headhunting you need to have excellent sales skills. On my first day, my direct boss gave me sheets of paper with the names of banks such as Goldman Sachs, Deutsche Bank, Morgan Stanley, Citibank, HSBC, Barclays to name a few. I think in total there must have been about 20 banks on my list to call in the cities of Tokyo, Hong Kong, and Singapore. My manager told me to call these banks and gather the names of people who worked in the IT department of the bank. That was it. At first it was very intimidating as I knew the other guys and the boss were potentially listening in, there was nowhere to hide. If I had done cold calling in the past, I would always prefer to do that from a private space.

If I was not on a call, I could listen in to the other guys when they made a call. I tried to pick up some of the lines they used to get past the bank's receptionists. The receptionists were like gatekeepers. It was not easy getting past them, they must have been briefed to be aware of recruiters or headhunters. When I started to make my calls, I would tell the receptionists that I was calling from Microsoft, Oracle, or some other well-known tech company, (using a fake name) and say that I needed to speak with someone in their IT department. My stories seemed to work most of the time. Once I was transferred to someone in IT, I took down their name, job title, and their direct phone number.

That was my brief, make calls and collect names. Nothing else. I must have made around 200 phone calls each day. I did this for two weeks straight. The owner of the company, Terry, had made millions in recruitment and he moved to Australia to focus on building the business in Asia using Australia as his base. If he sensed the office was a little too quiet, he would be on our case telling us to get on the phones. He was a bit of a slave driver at times, and he didn't have any sense of humour, and by any, I mean zero. I don't think I ever saw him smile either. He may have had money, but he seemed like a miserable bastard. If ever there was a case of money not making you happy, he would have been the poster boy for it.

Between calls we used to flick emails to each other as a bit of light entertainment. It was nothing more than harmless fun. But we enjoyed it as talking was basically banned during precious phone calling time. I was given a key to the office and would arrive at about 8.30 am. Most of the other guys came in around 9 or 9.30 am, and we could start making calls at 10 am as Tokyo and Hong Kong were behind us by two or three hours. After my two weeks of cold calling and collecting names, I was told to ring the people whose names I had collected. I was told to ask them if they were interested in an open position with another bank. This was the second part of my job, and this is called 'headhunting'.

Most people I spoke to were happy to have a conversation, and I would call them back after-hours for a more detailed conversation. Then if they agreed to be represented, I would get them to send me their resume and with their permission I would send the resume off to various IT managers. I kept making calls to find new candidates and at the same time I continued to build up a good relationship with these managers, who now started to send me open positions that they had. I was settling in nicely and enjoying the new career. I also started to have some candidates on the go doing the rounds for some roles that I picked up. I was now about three months in, and I had picked up the art of headhunting. This area of sales is not for everyone, but I enjoyed it. The potential to make some good money also excited me.

One Friday morning I came in to work at 8.30 am as usual and to my surprise I found Terry sitting at his desk. This was odd as he never came into work before me. I said good morning to him, and he grunted back at me. I didn't need to be a mind reader to tell he was really pissed off. I had no idea what had made him so mad, and I didn't really want to know either. Then I noticed all the computers had been turned on. That was odd. Obviously, Terry had turned on everyone's PCs and he had found something, but I didn't ask. If it had anything to do with me, I was certain I would find out later. I just let him marinate away in his own juices until he was ready to say something, if anything, I was worried he was going to explode.

The other guys started rolling in through the door and they looked at me quizzically. I just looked back at them, shrugged my shoulders with a look on my face that read 'I have no idea what's up with the boss'. Terry then went into one of the offices and he started this crazy inquisition. One-by-one, he started to call us into this office for some kind of interrogation. I had yet to be called in, so I still had no idea of what was happening. This had gone on all day, it was now 4 pm and it was my turn to be questioned. He called me into the office and asked me to close the door. He told me to take a seat, then he said, 'Explain this to me,' as he handed me a piece of paper.

It was an email and it read; *"Terry hasn't made a call in half an hour."*

It was one of the emails I sent to a workmate. I said to him, 'Look, it was a joke. We all work hard, and it was my attempt at humour.'

Obviously, Terry didn't have much of a sense of humour, he certainly didn't like the joke at his expense. My workmate foolishly forgot to delete this email, and I thought it was going to be much worse. Terry said, 'If you have got something to say, then say it to my face.'

I said, 'Terry, it was a joke,' I apologised to him, and reiterated, 'We work hard on the phones all day, and I meant no harm by it.'

Terry then said, 'You have done well so far, and you have got some good business in your pipeline, but I am going to have a think over the weekend and let you know on Monday if you have your job.'

BIPOLAR HEAD

I was in shock. Lose my job over this? He had to be kidding.

I then said, 'Terry, I like recruitment, and I am going to continue working in recruitment for you or someone else. Please have a think now because I would like to know before I leave this room if I have a job. I am not going to sweat it out over the weekend wondering if I have job next week.'

Terry thought about this for a minute and then said, 'Okay, you can stay.'

I left the room slightly rattled, but decided then that this was not going to work out for me. From that moment I knew I had to find another company to work for. The following week, Terry went overseas, and I managed to find a company that was happy to employ me. I was not entirely sure if I wanted to make the move yet, but I had all my contacts backed up on a spreadsheet, so I was ready to move.

Then I made a fatal error. I went for a coffee with my direct manager, the younger Londoner who I thought I could trust, and I told him that I was considering this move. I have no idea why I did this, but it was foolish. He said, 'Right, you're fired,' and just like that he marched me up to the office to grab my bag, and I was walked out of the office in front of everyone. What a prick. I couldn't believe it. It was the most embarrassing incident that has ever happened to me in a workplace.

I was not manic, just stupid. I wish I could blame my bipolar brain on this dumb move, but I couldn't. From a mental perspective, everything was going just fine. I was doing well at work thankfully, so I didn't do anything else stupid. Of course, I had thought of waiting for him after work. I just didn't like to be bullied or intimidated by the boss. Inside, of course I was angry with myself for opening my big mouth, and I felt like smashing him for sacking me, and embarrassing me in front of everyone, but I don't smash people, and I only had myself to blame. I went over to the office of the company I had interviewed with and told them I was ready to start the following week. I was starting over, but I was on a better deal as this company paid a 50/50 split of commission. The vibe in the office was better as well, it was much more relaxed. There was no crazy macho bravado.

I had to start from scratch finding new jobs and candidates for these jobs, but it didn't take long before I was doing well. While I didn't like the way I had been ejected and marched out of the office, in hindsight it was a good move. The three months I spent working for Terry taught me all the skills I needed to get my head around the art of headhunting. As for Terry, the only thing I have to say to him is, thank you for giving me the opportunity, and thank you for teaching me the skills of headhunting. I know that he was rewarded financially as I had a placement that I could not take with me to the new company and the fee for that placement was over eighty thousand dollars, so he got a return on his investment in me. Of course, 33-percent of that fee went to the guy who walked me out of the office, but I was in a better company, armed with the skills that they could not take off me, and now all I had to do was pick up the phone and make calls to hunt some more heads and find new jobs for these people.

CHAPTER 40
Along Came A Girl

Life was good. I was happy, and things were going well at the new recruitment company that I joined. I had been making some placements and the money for these placements started to come in. It was nice to be rewarded for the effort and it was also a confirmation that I was doing well in my new career. While I was still doing headhunting, this company also did short-term contract placements, and I worked closely with one of the other guys and together we found jobs and candidates for these shortterm roles which paid well.

My mental health was stable as well. I had not had any manias or depressions and I kept up my monthly appointments with my psych doctor who seemed to be very happy with me. It was a about a year and a half since my arrest and two-week vacation in Coffs Harbour. The meds my doctor had me on were keeping me stable, and that was the goal. When my mood was not up or down, it was what my doctor called euthymic. I was feeling good about myself, and I was happy. The one thing that I was missing in my life was a woman. Sometimes I would have an internal argument with myself that was negative, and I thought I didn't want to be a burden to anyone because of my bipolar, but I did miss having that special person in my life so why shouldn't I be able to have a relationship?

I was continuing along my spiritual path which also helped me to be grounded, so I started to look online at a Jewish dating site. I wrote to a few women with no luck and then I happened to find the profile of one woman who piqued my interest, so I contacted her. She wrote back to me about a day later. We continued to write to each other for a few days, then we decided to make contact for a chat on the phone. I gave her my number and she told me she would call me on Sunday night. I waited for her call, and she finally rang. We hit it off right away. I had no idea how the conversation was going to turn out, but it was effortless talking with her and we ended up talking for hours.

We decided to talk the next day and again we talked for about five hours. We had a great connection and planned to meet at a five-star hotel in the city the following Saturday. The week went by, and I set off to meet my internet date. I made it to the hotel a bit early, I had to calm myself down a bit, so I didn't seem so anxious. When she finally walked in through the huge glass doors to the lobby of the hotel, I was gobsmacked. She was gorgeous.

For a moment I thought that one of my friends must have been playing a joke on me, but thankfully this was not a joke, and our conversations continued effortlessly in person as well. This seemed way too good to be true. Her name was Rachel, and she was a lawyer. It had been such a long time since I met a down-to-earth Jewish woman who I got along with this well, and she seemed to feel the same way about me. We went to the hotel's restaurant and sat having dinner for three hours. Towards the end of the dinner, I said to her, 'There is something that you need to know about me.'

She asked, 'What is it?'

I told her that I have bipolar disorder. I was not sure how she was going to take this, but I felt I had to be honest with her right from the beginning, so I just put it out there not knowing how she was going to react. She asked me if I took my condition seriously, and I said, 'Of course, it is not a joke, I take it extremely seriously. I follow my doctor's instructions to the T; it is not a joke and can be very detrimental to my health if I don't take it seriously.' Rachel then said, 'So long as you follow your doctor's instructions to the letter then I don't have an issue. A friend of mine has bipolar, and I have seen her when she goes off her meds. She refuses to listen to her family and her friends, and then ends up spending time in a psych ward. I still love her as we go way back to our childhood but when she goes off her meds, she can be a handful.'

I said to Rachel, 'You're a good friend for sticking by her, but I want you to know I never go off my meds. I take my condition very seriously, I said. I have to.' I told her I had also been in a psych ward, and I pray to G-d that I never go there again.

We continued to date for about four months and then I asked her if she would like to move into my apartment. She said, 'Yes'. I was so happy, I just wanted to scream 'I'm the king of the world', I kissed her and told her how much I loved her. We arranged to meet the next day after I got some keys cut for her. I knew it was a bit fast, but I couldn't wait for her to move in.

It was now the middle of spring. A dangerous time for me for my bipolar mania making a cameo but things seemed to be fine. It was Wednesday evening and I asked Rachel if she would like to come join me for my consultation with my psych doctor the next day. She had not come with me before, and I thought as we were now a couple living together it would be good for her to sit in on one of my sessions with my brain care specialist. Rachel agreed to come along. My doctor never had any issues if I wanted to bring any family along and I knew he certainly wouldn't mind if I brought Rachel either. I felt it was important for her to have an open line of communication as well should she ever have any questions, and it was also good to have her hear what the doctor had to say when I presented myself to him. There were no secrets as far as I was concerned, and it was good that she met him just in case she wanted to ask him anything down the track.

CHAPTER 41
I Can't Believe My Ears

Things had been going along extremely well with Rachel and myself. We had been living together for about six months, and I have to say we were in love. But there was one major issue, and this potentially was a very serious problem for me. The problem was that her parents didn't like me. I can't say why they didn't like me, but they had their reasons. It wasn't the first time that my girlfriend's parents didn't like me. I copped the same BS from my ex-wife's parents. For some reason, I would only get this type of negativity from the parents of Jewish girls I dated. If I dated a non-Jewish girl, I was always welcomed into their home.

With regards to Rachel's parents, their disapproval of me may have been because I had been married before, or maybe it was because I was eight years older than her. One other reason may have been because I had a young daughter, who by the way, got on well with Rachel, or it may have been a combination of all these things, or some other reason. I don't know, but either way I felt their outward pouring of negativity towards me, and it was something that I was not going to tolerate.

I had only met her parents maybe two or three times, but with each visit, their cold shoulder treatment seemed to get worse and worse. I found both of her parents to be extremely rude to me, frankly, I just wanted to get out of their house within five minutes of being there. The thought of having to sit through dinner while having to fake pleasantries was painful. All I wanted to do was just cut and run. I didn't want to talk with them, and they didn't want to talk with me so let's be honest we should have just called the whole charade off.

I had experienced this before in another relationship and I am not going to state which one it was, but it was horrendous. Having to go through that, and having my partner put me second every time was horrible. It is one thing to be disliked by nonJews, but to be disliked by your own people is a whole different trip. It was nasty. I didn't want Rachel to have to choose between me and her parents, but I told her the only way our relationship would go the distance was if we left Sydney and set up our lives somewhere else. We could have gone anywhere but I suggested to her that Noosa Heads was a great place to consider. I fell in love with Noosa Heads when I went there on tour with the band. To me it seemed like a magical place with a warm subtropical environment and some of the best beaches and surf in Australia. Rachel agreed, and that was our goal.

I was working on a placement that potentially was going to be my biggest fee if it came in. The deal was worth seventy-five thousand dollars, and I would get half. The candidate had quite a few more interviews to go through, and I was not counting my chickens before they hatched, but if this deal came in, I was going to use my money to set up my own recruitment company. As my work was essentially all done on the phone, it didn't matter where I worked from. Rachel said she would be able to find a law firm to work for up on the Sunshine Coast, so she agreed to our plan for the sake of our relationship.

One Sunday, Rachel and I went along to see my daughter's tee-ball game. We were standing there at the game watching alongside the other parents, and my ex-wife and her parents were at the game as well. Suddenly, my ex-mother-in-law who was behind us started saying negative comments in Hungarian about myself and Rachel. This was because Rachel and I were holding hands and publicly displaying affection, not intentionally, but my exwife was also at the game. For this display of affection, I received a tirade of abuse, that no one else could understand unless they spoke Hungarian.

I could not believe what I was hearing. I'm looking at my daughter involved in the game in front of me, and I am hearing this talk coming from behind me. I thought I was having an auditory hallucination. My blood began to boil. I started to lose my mind and I just told Rachel we must leave, now. We got back in the car, and I drove us home, and the words would not leave my head. It was springtime and yes, I was in a slightly elevated headspace, but the words sent me over the edge.

I kept playing them over and over and this set off a mania on another level. The following day Rachel rang my psych doctor, and he agreed to see us. When we went to see my doctor, he couldn't believe my change in mood because when we had seen him three days earlier, I was fine and now I was extremely manic, in fact he said I was frightening. Now that is something I never want to be called again.

We went home and about 40 minutes later, the Community Health Team arrived at my apartment with the police, and I was taken away, yet again to my home away from home to cool my heels. Once again, I was given the red card and I copped a month for my bad attitude. Poor Rachel, she just didn't know what to do, but I am sure it was my psych doctor who told her to keep me at the apartment and he will arrange for the crisis team and the cops to come and collect me.

Of course, I was manic, and I was triggered by someone who in the past had been quite unpleasant towards me. I don't know why I just didn't walk away sooner when she started, but I didn't have the skills, awareness, or self-control that I have today, so they did what was best and that meant a bit of time in the cooler to bring my elevation down.

Rachel would come and visit me while I was locked up, but I could feel that she would be reconsidering our move away together. During my four-week stay, I managed to get a lot of coins for the payphone as mobile phones were not allowed. I called the office, and they gave me the numbers I needed to call, and after three weeks of being locked up, I got the best news. My candidate was offered the role. I was still inside the puzzle factory, but the candidate didn't know that. It would have to be the craziest job placement ever. I had no access to a computer, so I got the secretary to take over my email account from this point. She would be handling all the email correspondence with the bank and the candidate on my behalf. I would take care of the calls, and together we did what was required to make sure that the candidate and the bank were taken care of, and all the contracts were signed. It was the biggest fee I had done, and the biggest fee the company had ever billed, and I closed it all off while being locked inside the laughing academy.

Now that is nuts! As for the candidate, he was thrilled, and I told him he would be able to start as soon as he liked. He said he would like to start in two weeks, so the date was set. He gave notice and the deal was done. I was over the moon except for the fact that I was still in the laughing academy. I was now climbing the walls to get out. I told Rachel and she was very happy for me. But then she said that she was going to move out from my flat. I was devastated.

I told her, 'Look, I understand, and I can't blame you, but if you move out, I am still going to move to Noosa. I can't stand living here in Sydney. I am always being locked up in this town every other year, and I can't take being locked up against my will. It's just the people here, and the way they irritate me. I must find another place to live.'

With that she said, 'I still love you and I hope you find the peaceful place you are looking for.'

I looked in her eyes and could tell she still had feelings for me. She said she was sorry, but she just could not deal with having to go through another mania like that again. To be honest neither could I.

My heart was torn into a thousand pieces. But I knew what she felt, and that rage that came over me without the self-control to wind it down was just something that I had to learn to control. Many years later I would be able to control the raging Hulk, as I used to call it. But this time the Hulk got the better of me and frightened off the woman who I thought I was going to settle down with. I was sure her parents had a big say in her decision, so she had them to please and contend with, and from my point of view I could not stand the thought of marrying into a family (again) that treated me like some second-rate citizen. I was devastated.

My four weeks in the nut house were done, and it was time to come home. As usual, the mental brain sedation therapy worked well to bring my inflamed temper and bad attitude back to normal. If anything, at least I know the drill on how to survive in there and have a regime on what I need to do to help with the passing of time. It still goes slow, but at least I know how to play the game. In the laughing academy there is only one winner, them, but if you play your cards right and follow the rules you will get by without too much pain and suffering.

CHAPTER 42
She's Gone And So Am I

I was a free man now, out from my four weeks of unpaid leave, and I was bloated from all the medications that they had given me. There never is enough room in that place to exercise either so as usual I put on about 10 kilograms. I was lucky to have my mother pick me up and I was heading back to my apartment to see if Rachel had really done what she said she was going to do.

I opened the door and walked to the closet to see if her clothes were gone, and they were. She had been coming to feed the cat each day, and the only thing she had left for me was a note that said: 'I love you, and will always love you, I hope you find your happy place.'

Yep, she loved me but couldn't stand to be in the same room as me. And with that it was like a hundred knives had just ripped through my chest and torn my heart to bits. Standing in this flat, this place that was my happy place, especially with her, was now a place I just wanted to get away from.

I had work which was a good distraction, and I was waiting patiently for the money to come in from the placement of the candidate in Tokyo. Two weeks rolled past rather quickly, and the money came in. At least work was going well, and they were pleased to see me in the office every day. After work at night, I would head home to an empty flat. Correction, I did have the cat, so the flat was technically not empty. The cat was ours, but now it was just a permanent reminder of the relationship we shared. Maybe I should have given the cat to her, but she didn't really want it and it was my idea to get the minx, so in a way I was happy I got to keep her.

I didn't like heading home each night and I seemed to have forgotten just how bad a broken heart can make one feel. As I always say, there is a pill for heartburn but no pill for heartache. I was struggling without Rachel not being in my flat and in my life. Walking into that apartment each night was a reality check, and I hated it. Every night felt like a kick in the guts as I walked into my apartment. Sometimes I would wake in the middle of the night from a dream with her in it, only to find she was not beside me.

I finally got the payment for the placement in Tokyo and with that I told the company I was moving up to Queensland, I didn't want to live in Sydney any longer. I thanked them and wished them well. A few days later I got on a flight to the Sunshine Coast. I knew nobody there but felt that I was going to rebuild my life in this tropical paradise. I booked into the Sheraton on the main street of Noosa and went about looking for an apartment to rent. I was there about two weeks, and I had a great time. I was still very much broken on the inside, but nobody looking at me could tell, it was my secret, and I wasn't going to share.

There is something liberating about being in a new town not knowing anyone or nobody knowing you. Luckily people can't see that you are carrying a broken heart around. I think that added another 10 kilograms to the additional depression which had set in post mania, but I knew in my heart that this was the best place for me to heal.

I found a townhouse to rent in Sunshine Beach. It was an amazing part of Noosa, a bit out of the way from the main drag of Hastings Street which was the tourist trap, filled with hotels and expensive restaurants. Sunshine Beach had lovely little coffee shops and a few bars and restaurants as well, it had a wholesome village atmosphere. I told the agent (who in time would become a good friend of mine), that I will be back in a week. I signed the lease, flew back to Sydney, and bought a four-wheeled drive (4WD) from a friend of mine.

As I was going to rent out my flat, the friend who sold me the car asked if he could move in. I let it to him with my furniture in there, bed and all and he moved in the day I left to go back up to Noosa. I was still a shell of a man from the treatment in the laughing academy.

As usual, the hospital managed to bring my elevated mood under control, but I had gone from being manic to that sickening side of bipolar, yes, I was depressed. I was used to this cycle, but I didn't have the mastery that I have now to be able to snap out of the depression or just do what needs to be done to change my mood to a levelled state of mind. I also had my broken love-sick heart to deal with, and that just added to my depression. I was lower than I had even been in the past. It was not good, but I had to deal with it. I drove up to Noosa in one go, making a few stops along the way to rest. I was glad to be there in my townhouse.

I was 1,200 kilometres away from my ex, my family and I didn't know anyone, except for the real estate agent who I leased the flat from. He came over later that night and told me that there was some good coke in town. I wanted to get away from this and honestly thought I had left it all behind back in Sydney.

Drugs were not supposed to be a part of my new life here, in a way it was like G-d testing me. Well, it was the *Yetzer Hora*, the evil inclination that was doing the testing, and I weakened. Sure, let's get some. I thought it might help to numb the pain of my heartache. So much for my sobriety. I was kidding myself if I thought that drugs were not here in this sleepy town. I didn't even seek them out, they found me. The nasty evil inclination just had to test me, didn't it?

During that first week I had to force myself to get out of bed. I was very low, it was the downside of the mania, but I had to push myself, so I would get up and go for a walk along the beach. The beach was spectacular. It went for miles and miles in one direction to Coolum, the other way led to the headland of North Sunshine. Australia's beaches are magnificent. It's hard to say whether one beach is better than another but walking on the sand with the warm subtropical waters lapping at my feet, I was getting better one day at a time.

I set up my recruitment company and called it Pacific International Recruitment. I had my moments when I felt good enough to pick up the phone and hunt for new roles, and then there were other days where I felt it was all too much and I just had to stay in the game of life as a survivor, praying for my mood to lift. Staying in bed watching movies or sleeping helped to pass my time with this depression. It always does. There is no need to give myself a hard time when I am in this mood either. I just have to let myself go with the flow but promise that tomorrow I will be getting up and doing what I need to do, walk, get in the water, and get on the phones to make some calls.

About every four weeks I would come back to Sydney to see my daughter and my mother. This went on for about three months. I was still very much in love with Rachel, and we kept in contact by the phone. It was after these phone calls that the pain seemed to intensify, I just wished we were still together. Break out your violin, here comes the good bit. I asked her out on a date the next time I was to be in Sydney, and she agreed to come to dinner with me. I came back to Sydney, and we went out for a fantastic Japanese dinner at our favourite restaurant. Then after dinner I asked her if she wanted to come back to my place and she did. She stayed the night, it was fantastic. I felt like the battery in my body had been replaced and I was reenergised. In the morning she went off to work. I went over to my flat. I sat down and the guy renting the flat from me seemed anxious. He asked me about the dinner date with Rachel and I told him that I think it went well. She came back to my place after.

Then he had this nervous look in his eyes, he said, 'I have to tell you something.'

I had no idea what he was about to say, and then he dropped a bomb on me. He said that he had been having an affair with Rachel. I could not believe what I was hearing. I mean technically we had broken up, but how could she sleep with him? And how on earth could he do this dirty act of betrayal on me, his mate, and the thought of him doing this in my bed, was just off the hook.

I was totally beside myself and could not work out who did the ultimate act of betrayal. Well, I suppose neither as technically Rachel and I were not an item. I went and got a bottle of Jack, as this was way too much for me to handle. The booze did help a bit, but I felt betrayed by both of them.

When I finally got around to seeing Rachel, I asked her, 'Why him? You could have slept with any man, you're a gorgeous, intelligent woman. You could have any man. Why did you have to sleep with him? Be honest and tell me why!'

Her answer was simple. She said, 'I did it because you went away, you left me.'

I said to her, 'I told you if you move out of the flat, I am still going to move to Noosa. I was still going away, so you had to punish me by sleeping with him.'

'Yes,' she said, 'I did. It was revenge.'

I could not believe those words were coming out of her mouth. She actually said that. It was an act of revenge. I'm lucky she didn't put the cat in a pot and boil it to death. This was now a bit too much for me to deal with, looking back in hindsight, he did me a favour. Call me old fashioned but if there is no loyalty then there really is nothing.

Who knows, if we had stayed together, down the road she may have applied a bit of her revenge at some other time.

It was brutal, but now she handed me a good reason to remove the rusty barb she left in my heart and leave this city that seemed to be a such a huge source of recurring pain.

So there ended the story of Rachel.

I went back to my new home on the Sunshine Coast, happier than when I left. At least now I had some closure on that relationship, and it made things feel a little bit better. I had not shaken off the depression but it was getting better day by day.

CHAPTER 43
It's Not The End Just The Beginning

Moving to Noosa was the best thing that I did. I couldn't live in Sydney anymore. I felt like I was a marked man with the police. They and the Community Health Team had my name on a list as someone who may be a danger to myself or someone in the community. Not a great list to be on because if anyone made a complaint against me, they would be there with numbers to haul my arse away.

It was relieving to be in a small, friendly community where I wasn't stigmatised or judged because of my bipolar. I was waking up in paradise every day. I still had some emotional scars from the way my relationship had ended, and my last round at the puzzle factory, but time heals most things and six months seemed to fly by and by then I had Rachel out of my head.

I started my days with a walk on the beach, followed by coffee and some breakfast at one of the local cafés. Then I would do some work for a few hours followed by a surf or if there were no waves I would jump into the water for a swim. I had a great neighbour who was a professional photographer. We hit it off and would go out for dinners or have home-cooked meals and we took turns cooking.

It was a new chapter in my life, and there were lots of adventures to come. The year was 2002 and if you told me that in five years' time, I would be off to America to run an IT start-up business in Phoenix, Arizona, I would have asked you what the hell have you been smoking? Are you out of your mind? But that's exactly what happened. Mike my dear friend who I worked with in 2000 had a new technology and he asked me if I wanted to run the business for him. At the same time, I was headhunted by another recruitment firm who wanted to buy my business and then send me to Hong Kong to run their office over there. It is weird how things go, one minute you get a great opportunity and then out of the blue, another great opportunity comes along and now I had to decide.

I think financially I would have been better off if I had sold my business and taken the role in Hong Kong. But I was always fascinated with the USA, and the lure of working there was just too strong, so after six fun years in Noosa, I came back to Sydney for a while to learn about the technology Mike had put together. I was the third employee in the company and after five months in

Sydney, Mike, one of his tech guys and I flew over to Phoenix to set up the company.

I ended up working there for seven years. I took the business through the great crash of 2008, and we survived that, although a lot of businesses over there didn't. I thought that the job working with Mike was going to be my last job, but I ended up getting shafted and I knew that the 'you're going to get screwed' card was in that deck. It was not so much Mike, as it was his partners. I was on a great salary, but I was always being promised a percentage, which ended up being just that, a promise.

In the back of my mind, I kind of saw it coming, it was a hard job. But I loved the challenge. It's one thing going to the States on holiday but working there was brutal. It's a tough market, and we had lots of competition. After I got the short stick, and was told that I was going to be micromanaged – it was the last straw for me. I had started that business from scratch and took their eighthundred-thousand-dollar investment to profit. The business is still going well today, so I am proud of the legacy I left behind. I also made some dear friends, who I love, and I still talk to them to this day.

I also knew I had to come home to look after my ageing mother. I was one year away from getting my Green Card and I would have loved to have stayed. Americans love Aussies, and in a way it felt like being a minor celebrity. They just loved to hear the Aussie accent. The big difference is this: in Australia, I would be classified or called a 'wog', in America I was an Australian. If you don't know what a 'wog' is, it's a derogatory word for anyone with Mediterranean features. Today, I think some of the racist people of Australia sadly don't understand that it's time to grow up.

Regarding my great job, I felt that it was time to come home, and the BS that Mike and his partners were putting on me was not fair. I rang my lawyer, and he said I was nuts as I had a year to go and I would have my Green Card, but I had my responsibility to my mother. I had no siblings and she needed me back home. She was now 90, still strong, but she missed me and I her.

I fell on my sword and took the years' salary that I was offered and came back to Australia. Back to North Bondi in the pretentious Eastern Suburbs of Sydney, which was a respectable workingclass suburb now mature and all grown up. All of a sudden the suburb of Bondi Beach was now a land of show-offs and dickheads. The money wanted to be close to the beach and the city, and land was at a premium. These blow in peeps with their fresh attitudes and leased European cars thought the sun shines out of their asses. It was not a friendly atmosphere anymore. I hated being back in Sydney. Yes, I had my obligation to fulfil, but I think I was depressed for two years. It was hard settling back in.

I also had moments when I was pushed by certain people with their entitled attitude, or those that did not realise when my moods turned to mania and they just made me angry and pushed my buttons till I exploded. It was a brutal time for me.

When I did manage to get out from my depression, and spring would roll around I would find that I would end up back at the puzzle factory every other year for my crimes of moral turpitude.

There was one siege at my house after I posted something on Facebook, obviously it was not a socially acceptable comment. This inflamed the community health people who had been alerted to my words, and they came over with the police. I refused to go with them and barricaded myself in my bedroom.

I had no idea how many police were at my house. When I say I was barricaded in my bedroom, I had just pushed a chair against the door. The door didn't even have a lock on it. But I was not coming out. I wasn't being a hard-ass, I just refused to go with them. I told them to get the doctor to make a house call but that wasn't going to happen.

The female police negotiator was doing her best and assured me that she was going to get me out. I told her fine, but I'm still not walking out. She assured me that they would get me out. Brilliant. Break out the teargas and smoke grenades. Luckily for me that didn't happen.

They burst through my bedroom door, three cops, two with tasers drawn one pointed at my head the other pointed at my chest. 'GAME OVER!', I shouted. The female cop negotiator who was the third cop, said, 'Hands behind your back!'

When I walked out of my house it was like the final scene from *Rambo: First Blood*. There were cops everywhere, three on the carport looking at how to break into my bedroom window, another six just standing around as backup. I could not believe all this attention was just for me. Who the hell did they think I was?

I think in total there were 10 cops just for me! Did they think I was Australia's most wanted?

As you might guess I got four weeks in the can again. It was the usual business of the puzzle factory, and after complying with their ways, my manic brain was filled with peace and tranquillity. I think that round taught me a lot about being back in Sydney. I just had to be on my best behaviour at all times.

It was the hardest decision I had to make coming back, leaving a great job to come back to look after my mother, but I did. I also learnt a lot about my bipolar manias which when they arrived each spring, I just accepted them and learnt that I just had to stay home medicated up to the eyeballs, so that I was not being a bipolar maniac. I have since learnt the hardest lessons this condition has thrown at me, and that is to just stay at home and take my meds until it blows over, when the mania is out of my system, then I can be ready to engage in society.

Bipolar has been my life's biggest challenge. In a way it is a game I have had to play against myself. I have had to learn some of the hardest lessons over and over, I think that is how it had to be sadly, but to be where I am today, I can say that I am in a happy place.

Again, because my manic brain was just so charged at times and I had such a lack of insight, or the right medications I had no way to control it. Learning about myself, and my moods of bipolar, and how to deal with these moods have been the challenge that I would like to think I now know how to handle, and how to control. Thanks to medication and self-awareness.

So many times, in the past I just didn't behave well. It has taken me a lifetime of lessons to know what I know about myself now, and how to behave. Along the way there have been friends that I have lost, and family that I have upset and hurt, for that I am truly sorry.

But the best friends I have today stayed the distance, and accepted me for who I am, and I love you both dearly. Of course, I am joking there are a few more, but you know who you are, and I love you for putting up with me during times when I have pushed you to the point of sheer frustration. For that I am forever grateful.

I just want to say that bipolar has been challenging but then again, any illness or health condition can be. Bipolar has not defined me, and it never will. But I have learnt to live with it and deal with it when my moods just fly in one direction or the other. Thank goodness that I have the medication and a great psych doctor who cares, and with these tools it certainly helps me to live a happy life.

My experiences have been fun, sometimes crazy, and at other times hell, but I am still here in the game of life, and blessed to get up each day, no matter which way my brain is spinning.

CHAPTER 44
Some Loving Words...

The year we travelled to the States was 1988. It was my first trip to the States with my dear friend who wrote:

A manic and a depressive travel together.

The depressive uses alcohol and marijuana to mask his pain.

The manic uses cocaine to leave earth's orbit, alcohol to stay in touch with earth, and marijuana to re-enter.

They're due to meet at the depressive's apartment three hours before their flight leaves for LA. The depressive is anxious four hours before. The manic has a loose association with time, and the depressive knows it.

Two hours before they're due to travel, and the depressive is certain that all is lost. Any more implosive, and he will spontaneously combust.

100 minutes before take-off, manic shows up in the taxi, oblivious.

As the taxi heads down the main artery to the airport, they have 80 minutes to take off, and 20 minutes to drive.

'Just pull over here mate' manic says to the cab driver.

Depressive lets loose with every emotion he's been barely subduing.

'I'll just be a sec', don't worry' manic says.

Eight minutes is enough time for depressive, a chef, to make a soufflé. It feels like forever.

Manic comes out of the terrace; it's a dilapidated hole of a place, towels for curtains, barring any light, or eyes from entering. Suss doesn't begin to describe it.

Manic is furious as the cab resumes his dash to the airport:

'Fuck!' He says.

'What?' Depressive enquires.

'I was supposed to pick up 100 quaaludes, but they weren't there.'

Depressive is a black hole of catastrophizing. No light is getting out.

'I have two problems with that,' he explains, 'one is that we are travelling together, and US jail is not on the itinerary. The other is that you are smuggling quaaludes to the home of quaaludes... it makes no fucking sense!'

Of course, somehow, they make that flight, and the connection to New York, where the first thing depressive best friend's wife offers them is... yep, quaaludes.

As dysfunctional as this start was, it was to be a repetitive narrative of the trip.

Depressive wanting to get stoned and stay in his room. Manic dragging him out with his friends, similarly, buoyed by the marching powder... until finally, depressive "forces" manic to smoke some pot, so they can be at some sort of level together.

They miss planes when manic goes to the airport bathroom... for 30 minutes.

They miss fun when depressive hides inside himself and doesn't come out.

Somehow, they make it home, friends for life.

If this book raises any issues for you, please contact Lifeline or the relevant support services:

Lifeline 13 11 14 lifeline.org.au

Beyond Blue 1300 22 4636 beyondblue.org.au

Black Dog Institute (02) 9382 4530 blackdoginstitute.org.au

Emergency Services 000

www.ingramcontent.com/pod-product-compliance
Lightning Source LLC
Chambersburg PA
CBHW051305120626
46547CB00015B/2098